THE NEXT LEVEL:

A Game I Had To Play!

by

Vernon Maurice Turner

THE NEXT LEVEL:
A Game I Had To Play!

ISBN-13: 978-0-9844736-1-8

Book Layout Design:
Gianna Carini
www.brighteyes.org

Original Cover Design:
Dawud West for Darkness Bros. Inc.
www.cargocollective.com/Darknessbros.com

Cover Design Edits (for size/content):
Gianna Carini

Printed in the United States of America.

First Edition - 2010.

Dedication

This book is dedicated to my mother, Jackie, and my father, Sam. I never realized all the sacrifices the two of you made for me, Jemal, Sharlene, Brian, and Ellen. It wasn't until I actually started writing this book that I discovered all that you did for us.

Mom, you made an unthinkable sacrifice for me back in 1966. I truly hope that you are able to read this book from above, because I want you to know that I love you with all my heart, and that I am truly heartbroken by the way we left things.

Dad, it wasn't until the last two years of your life that I made you feel wanted and needed by me. Like Mom, it wasn't until I started writing this book that I truly realized the amount of sacrifices you made for all of us. Because of my ignorance, I missed out on so many years with you; you are one incredible man and I am extremely proud to call you my father! This is something I should have said twenty four years ago... I love you, Dad!

THE NEXT LEVEL:

A Game I Had To Play!

by

Vernon Maurice Turner

Table of Contents

Fourth Quarter

Introduction

Today is December 10, 2009. My name is Vernon Turner and, strangely enough for me, I have a story to tell. Why is this so strange for me? I guess you might say the reason is because anyone that knows me will agree when I say I am a very private person. I keep my personal affairs under lock and key. For me, this book and a project of this magnitude represents something extremely uncharacteristic and completely outside of my comfort zone.

It's safe to say that everyone has a story to tell—you probably even have one of your own. Some life stories are sprinkled with tragic events, some with extremely dysfunctional pasts, and some are downright inspirational. The story you will read in the following pages has all of these things. It has taken me well over sixteen years to be "okay" with following through with this project. The people closest to me are going to be shocked as hell to see me exposing my life in the form of a book.

While telling my story, I hope to give a clear enough insight of what my world was like from age five to the present, and it is my sincere hope that this story will touch and inspire all those who read it.

In some ways I consider myself a pretty deep person. I tend to analyze and dissect everything: my past, present, and future; all the decisions I've made; and all the things I've done, whether good, bad, or indifferent. All of it has made me the man I am today. It's scary for me to think about how it all started and it has been one hell of a ride. During my journey, some unbelievable individuals have crossed my path. You will read here about a handful of people that were extremely instrumental in the outcome of who and where I am now. If I had to choose a few words to describe my story, they would have to be sadness, embarrassment, touching, heartbreak, guilt, regret, anger, fear, determination, and relief. What amazes me is that I remember it all like it was yesterday!

First Quarter

My grandmother, Alene. RIP.

Chapter 1:
Life in Brooklyn

I grew up in Bedford Stuyvesant, Brooklyn, New York. I remember living in my grandmother's house with a crap-load of cousins. Nana's house was never empty and that is not mere exaggeration. It started off with me and my brother, Jemal. If you know anything about 1970s Bedford Stuyvesant ('Bed-Stuy' to the locals), you know it wasn't an ideal place to live. Looking back now, I think Bed-Stuy got a bad rap. Unfortunately, many areas predominately Black (African-American) and economically challenged are labeled 'bad' or 'unsafe.' Like any other place, if we minded our own business and didn't start any trouble, life was good. If we looked for trouble or messed with someone or their family member, then 'consequences' were gift-wrapped and personally hand delivered. For me, that's where our home was, and that's all we knew at the time... and that made it okay for us.

I remember playing outside of 465 Herkimer Street, our address in Brooklyn. Back then, we played right in the middle of the street, particularly my all-time favorite, 'Skully'—a street game I was pretty much addicted to as a kid. It was a pretty popular game because it was affordable. The game consisted of a big ol' six-foot by six-foot box placed in the middle of the street. Besides that, all we needed was a bottle cap, maybe a little wax or anything that would weigh the cap down, and some chalk, and the game was on. I remember playing Skully when I was about six years old. The traffic on that side of town was pretty heavy, so we had to dodge cars during the game. We had a person to look out for cars while we played, and that person was usually someone's mother, sister, or girlfriend. Whenever one of our lookouts yelled, "Car!" everybody would scatter. Those were great times. Stickball and handball were really big back then, too. I don't particularly remember playing any of the more common sports like basketball or football during that time, but I was big on street games.

The Brooklyn winters were extremely cold, and the summers were extremely hot. We didn't have a pool in our back yard, nor did we have any place to go to borrow one. The one thing we had going for us back then was that we were big on improvising. Even though we didn't have a swimming pool to cool off in, we did have fire hydrants. One of the parents or one of the older kids would get one of those big ol' wrenches and open up the hydrant cap and increase the water pressure, and, man, talk about fun! It was more fun than any run-of-the-mill swimming pool.

I had a very close-knit family back then. No one messed with the Murph family, especially our women. They didn't need their brothers to protect them; they took care of themselves and distributed their own fair share of justified butt-kicking around our neighborhood to both men and women. The men in our family were highly respected, for they also refused to take crap from anyone. My mother was the third youngest of ten children—yes, TEN!—So you can imagine the number of cousins I had. My grandmother's house was a substation for all the grandkids. You would think so many kids around all the time would drive a little old lady to drink herself into a coma, but Nana loved having us around.

My aunts and uncles were always respectful, polite, and extremely kind to everyone they came in contact with. They would always go out of their way to help anyone in need. It didn't matter if the person needed food, clothes, money, or a place to lay their head, my family always reached out to help. This was something they got from my grandmother, the Grand Poobah of grandmothers. I can't even count the times Nana brought in a hungry, lonely stranger off the street to feed them. Everyone knew my grandmother in our neighborhood.

I remember once when I was walking home from the grocery store with Nana. We noticed two teenage boys fighting and throwing punches and they were some pretty big dudes (but then, I was only six years old, so everyone looked pretty big to me). In any case, they each towered at least two feet over my little nana. I remember her telling me to go inside a check-cashing place nearby, and then she went over to where they were fighting. Now, my grandmother was about five-two, 115 pounds, soaking wet, but she had the voice of someone six-three and 300 pounds. I stood in that check-cashing place, with our groceries beside me, watching my grandmother approach the knuckleheads. I was so scared for her that I was about to run home and get my cousins, but Nana told me to stay put, and I wasn't one to disobey her. My hands were pressed up against the glass that place and I was saying to myself, "Why doesn't someone go over there and help my nana?" Those two guys were really going at it. Punches were being thrown every which way, and Nana was about to walk right into it!

I truly don't know what was going through her mind while she was making her way to them, but she never broke her purposeful stride. She got about five feet from them, and the next thing I heard was, "Stop that damn fighting!" You could have heard it from a half mile away.

I guess one of the boys saw who it was from the corner of his eye, because he immediately stopped mid-swing of throwing another punch. The other boy tried to throw a sucker punch, but Nana physically pushed him back, and that's when I saw a few of the older men making their way over to assist. Hell, my nana didn't need those fools! By the time those men got over there, she practically had the boys shaking hands. I don't know what else she said to them, but whatever it was, it calmed both of them down pretty quick.

Nana had such a way with people that it's hard to describe. She solved more problems in and outside of our family than I can count. Nana was my heart; she was the last person I saw before going to sleep and the first person I saw when I woke up. She was also by far the best cook on this planet. Family, friends, and even strangers paid her to make her fried chicken or pork chops for them. You might browse through some cooking magazine and see meals that look delicious, but chances are, those are just airbrushed and touched up and don't taste half as good as they look. My grandmother, on the other hand, really deserved her own cooking show, because her meals tasted exactly the way they looked: mouth-wateringly delicious! I can't recall one meal I didn't love, and I wasn't the only one that felt that way about my nana's cooking. We couldn't wait for the block parties, because that's when she really 'did her thang.'

The block parties we had were the best ever. Everybody chipped in, and there were always DJs and lots of food. The adults played cards and dominos, and all of us kids were busy with every street game you can think of. Everyone had mad love for one another during those block parties. Yeah, those were the good times.

But I also remember the not-so-good times. I saw gang fights right outside my window. We always knew ahead of time when a big fight was going to happen because we heard the older kids talking about it days before, and then it got to the adults. When that time came, all the kids had to be in the house so we didn't get hurt. One time, my nana called for me and my cousins to come inside because she had heard there was going to be some major fighting going on. She told us to close the curtains and get away from the window, but we always found a way to sneak a peek through one of the upstairs windows.

It was crazy. There would be no one in the street one minute, and in the next, we would see about fifty to sixty people coming down from one side of the street. Moments later, there would be fifty to sixty from the other side. There was always a lot of threatening and trash-talking as they approached each other. Then, when they got within twenty to thirty yards from one another, our grandmother would inevitably catch us snooping, and we would all be placed in our bedroom until it was over. The only thing we knew was what we heard the following day. From what I remember, the only good thing about those fights was that they fought with their fists (with the exception of a few bats and knives). It was a far cry from the way street fights are now, when they rely on guns like cowards. For the most part, though, I was pretty much protected and sheltered from all of that stuff. I didn't know too much of anything. I didn't know what was really happening and what was really going on with my family.

When I was about nine or ten, I discovered that my mom was heavily into drugs. She was a drug addict and used to work the streets. My grandmother was the nucleus of the whole family, and if anything went wrong we went to Nana's house, and that was that. She had good morals and values, so it was difficult to understand how and why my mother was doing what she was doing. That's how things were for my brother and me growing up in Brooklyn.

There were a lot of things I didn't understand back in the day, including why I was really staying with my grandmother. My brother and I stayed there with Nana and very rarely even saw our mother because she was never home. It was sad that she was out wasting her life, working the streets and using drugs, because my mom had been a pure athlete as a teenager, a big-time track runner. But then, something went tragically wrong with her.

I never knew my real father, and I never really questioned who he was. I knew my mom had dated someone named Edward Turner. At one point, she did marry him, though they got divorced shortly thereafter. That's how my surname, Turner, came to be. My mom's maiden name was Murph (also the last name my brother used). It always left questions in my mind, but some questions in life inevitably go unanswered.

I was five years old in this photo.

Chapter 2:
The Big Move to Staten Island

I really didn't know my mother all that well back then, as most of my time was spent with my grandmother and my cousins. I can't believe I remember this far back, but I do recall at age five calling my mother by her first name. I remember crying out, "Where's Jackie? I want Jackie." My mother lived with us, but she was always out doing something else. At age six, I didn't ask too many questions; hell, I didn't know what was really going on. All I knew was that my baby brother, my mother, and I were living in my grandmother's house. I knew it was my nana's house because whenever my mother and grandmother argued, Nana would remind my mother that she was living in her house.

I'm not sure if my mother ever graduated from high school, but I know that while she was in school, she was on the school track team and was known for being extremely fast. She also participated in the marching band and was known for her smile, for she had a smile that could light up the darkest of rooms.

I remember waking up in the middle of the night to my grandmother and mom arguing. I really wasn't too concerned about it because Mom and Nana got into it often, so I just turned over and went back to sleep. The following night, out of the blue, my mom came home and told me we were moving. I asked her where we were moving to, and she said, "Staten Island," that we were moving in with her boyfriend. I was only six and a half years old at the time and thought that maybe my memory had escaped me, but I didn't think I had ever met or laid eyes on any guy my mother had been seeing as a 'boyfriend.'

At first, I thought my mom was just talking, exaggerating just to piss my nana off; never in a million years would I have thought she would actually go through with it. I mean, nothing was being packed and I didn't hear anyone in the family talking about us moving. I think my mom knew how upset I was going to be because she packed up all of our things the night before we were scheduled to leave, while I was asleep.

To say I did not want to go would be an understatement of mass proportions. When the time came for us to move, I was kicking, screaming, and holding on to my grandmother. The only place I knew was Herkimer Street—465 Herkimer Street. That was my home. My grandmother tried to calm me down to get me to go along with the plan, and for the most part she did help a little bit—at least until my mom's boyfriend, Sam, drove up to the front of the house. As I mentioned earlier, I couldn't recall meeting or even laying eyes on any of the guys my mom was with, so you can imagine my surprise when I saw a White guy step out of the car!

My brother was only four years old at the time, and he really didn't know what was happening, so like any naïve pre-schooler, he ran to the car and jumped right in the back seat. I, on the other hand, had to be escorted by my grandmother. I was crying uncontrollably, and I wouldn't let go of Nana! She just kept talking to me and telling me everything was going to be okay. Once I finally got in the car, my grandmother placed the seatbelts on me and my brother. I still had a pretty good cry going on, but my grandmother did something that calmed me down almost instantly: She closed the passenger door and went over to Sam (my mother's boyfriend) and greeted him with a huge hug and smile, as if she had known him for years. The second I saw that, I stopped crying. I figured that if Nana trusted him and was happy to see him, Sam couldn't be all that bad. As quickly as I calmed down, I got upset all over again once the car drove away from the house. I was being stripped from the only home I knew, and I already missed my grandmother.

Ironically, my mother had met this Sam while working the street; I guess you could say he was a John. But it was obvious he saw something in my mother other than a one-night stand, because he ended up asking my mom to move in with him.

If you know anything about Staten Island, you know it is about 90 percent Caucasian, while Bedford Stuyvesant, Brooklyn, is probably about 98 percent African-American. Back then, I was taught not to trust White people, even though I was never taught to hate or dislike anyone. I remember just before leaving my nana's house, a few of my cousins pulled me aside and told me to watch what

I said or did around White people because "they don't like our kind." I asked my cousins why Whites didn't like us, and they said it was because we are a different color. They warned me to watch my back and my brother's too. My cousins told me if I ever needed them, just call. You can imagine how frightened I was after hearing that!

So there I was, a Brooklyn kid, being moved from my environment and my race to an area completely different than what I was used to. We moved to a neighborhood called Sunnyside on Staten Island—Glenwood Avenue, to be exact. I believe the year was 1973. As we drove into the neighborhood, I did not see one Black person—not a single one. My cousins had tried to prepare me, but to actually see it for myself was an experience in itself. I also noticed that all the houses had grass and trees, and the yards were like something I'd never seen except in magazines or on TV. The grass was perfectly cut, the hedges were trimmed, and there was not a single piece of trash on the ground.

When I first walked in the house, I just looked around in awe of where I was standing. I didn't move. I stood in the middle of the living room and surveyed the room with my eyes, taking it all in. Everything was in order, not a thing out of place. There were no marks on the walls, the carpet looked new, and the furniture looked well kept. Until that time, I'd never been in a White person's house, so I was really analyzing everything. I mean, I even noticed the difference in how his house smelled. It wasn't bad, just different.

Sam, my new stepdad, seemed okay. I noticed that he talked extremely loudly and that he was a decent-sized man, and I had no intention of pissing him off anytime soon.

I remember crying myself to sleep that first night. My mom kept trying to point out all the good things to me, like having my own bed to sleep in, staying in a really nice house, staying outside later because the neighborhood was safer and had better schools. Still, the only thing I heard coming out of her mouth was "blah, blah, blah…" I wasn't listening to one word she was saying; I was so angry with her. She could have had a roomful of toys waiting for me there, and it wouldn't have made a difference. I was a very unhappy little boy.

I remember going to school for the first time—I believe it was second grade—at Public School 35. I was extremely uncomfortable and reserved at first. I didn't trust the teachers, and I barely spoke to the staff or the other kids.

I was extremely upset with my mother for stripping me of the only home I knew. My beloved grandmother had raised me and my brother up to that point, and I didn't know my mother like I knew my grandmother. I mean, I knew she was my mother, but she wasn't around that much. Before Staten Island, I was almost always with my nana. To make matters worse, my new stepdad was someone I really didn't get along with at first. I didn't like him mainly because he argued with my mother all the time, and I also distrusted him because he was White. My mother had just sprung this guy on us. I didn't even remember meeting him prior to moving into his home. I resented my mother for taking me away from my family in Brooklyn, and I resented Sam just for being White. I was pissed off at the world, and at that time, no one could get through to me. Every time I spoke to my grandmother on the phone, I would just start crying and beg her to come and get me. This was a major adjustment for me. Like I said before, I was mad at the world. It got so bad for me during the first year that I thought about running away several times, but I was too scared to actually do it.

It didn't take long for my mom to begin reproducing again. It started off with me and my brother, Jemal, and then a year later we had a baby sister named Sharlene. Less than a year after that, our brother, Brian, popped out, and two years after that, my sister, Ellen, made her grand entrance to this crazy world. By the time it was all said and done, I had four siblings: two brothers and two sisters.

Chapter 3:
Major Adjustments

My early years on Staten Island were rough, to put it lightly. I had to get accustomed to a new way of living and a new outlook on things. Even though it was a better neighborhood with less crime, it didn't change the fact that there were no Black people—except us. We were the first Blacks to move into the neighborhood, and it raised a lot of Caucasian eyebrows. I didn't have any major issues with the neighborhood kids who were my age, but the teenagers really gave me a hard time.

I enjoyed playing Skully and missed it, so I tried to teach some of the neighborhood kids to play, but the homeowners there didn't take too kindly to people drawing chalk lines in the middle of the street. The first time I did it, the neighbors complained to my mom. She explained to them that it was just chalk and just a game and wasn't causing any harm. My mom didn't want to garner any more negative attention than what we were already getting, though, so she told me not to play Skully in the street anymore. The only time I got to play my favorite game was when I went to visit my family in Brooklyn, which wasn't often enough as far as I was concerned.

I remember this one high school kid that lived right next door to us. He hated me with a passion. He would stick his middle finger up at me and whisper, "Nigger, go away," every time he drove by. I can admit now that I was really afraid of the guy; I knew if he were able to do something bad to me and get away with it, he would do it. In fact, something bad did almost happen. I lived on the level portion of Glenwood Avenue, and to get to my house, we had to drive up a hill, and then the street leveled out. From where my house was, we could look to the right and see the peak before it went downhill to the bottom of the street. My house was approximately 50 to 60 yards from that peak. Even if someone was driving over the speed limit, they would have plenty of time to see whoever was in the street and slow down. This one particular time, a few other kids and I were playing two-hand touch football in the street. We all heard a car coming, so we stopped the game and moved to the side. I was standing on one side of the street, and the rest of the kids were on the other. When I saw the car approaching, I realized who it was, and I backed up even further, almost to the sidewalk. When he saw me, he proceeded to increase his speed to try to run me over. I literally had to jump onto the sidewalk to keep from getting hit.

That wasn't the last run-in I had with that individual. I came home from school one day and saw that someone had written in chalk on my driveway, "Nigger, go away." I knew who wrote it because he always whispered the exact same words every time he drove by me. I didn't say anything about it to anyone because I thought it would just make matters worse, but it reminded me of what my cousins had told me before I left Brooklyn. They were right to give me a heads up, and this guy's behavior wasn't too much of a surprise to me, but it did piss me the hell off. This, in turn, only made me more withdrawn.

As time went on, things did get better. I really couldn't complain too much in regards to school. The teachers were very nice to me, always extra helpful and willing to lend an extra helping hand. I believe they understood the transition I was going through, which made me more receptive to them. They never gave me a hard time about my many mood swings and just kept saying they were there for me. Eventually, they got through to me, and as a result, I ended up transitioning pretty well.

I even started taking part in recreational school sports like kickball, dodge ball, and tag. The important thing was that I was interacting, and I was turning into a pretty decent athlete along the way. Back then, my favorite sport was boxing. I was a big-time Muhammad Ali fan, and no one could tear me away from an Ali fight on TV. I remember looking in the newspapers and waiting for upcoming boxing events. I liked football, too, but I wasn't really into it like I was boxing.

Thinking back now, I can specifically remember when football really became an interest of mine, probably when I was about ten or eleven years old. When I wasn't babysitting my brothers and sisters, I'd try to sneak to Clove Lakes Park to play two-hand touch or tackle football with the neighborhood kids. Sometimes we would sneak onto the Wagner College game field and play there. Thank God for speed, because I didn't have the size. I don't think I ever realized how small I actually was, but when we played tackle football, even when they actually got a hold of me, they couldn't tackle me. It was the strangest thing—something you'd probably have to see to believe—and because of it, I was never picked last for teams. Everybody wanted me.

Here I am in 3rd grade. Yes, my mom had a thing for bowties!

Chapter 4:
A Grown-Up Childhood

During my elementary and middle school days, I knew my mom was heavily into drugs, and this made our home life difficult. She even took drugs while she was pregnant with three of my siblings, and shooting up with heroin cocaine was frequently her high of choice.

There were a lot of times when Mom was so wigged out on drugs that I would have to care for my brothers and sisters by myself. I had to cook, clean, change diapers, and watch over them because my mom had no problem relying on me as an in-house, built-in babysitter. Some days, my mom would get sick because of the drugs, and then I had to take care of her in addition to my brothers and sisters. Because I was so tied up taking care of things at home, participating in organized team sports was nearly impossible for me.

In spite of her own problems, my mom was extremely strict on us, and she was particularly hard on me. At the time, I didn't really understand why. I was often left home to watch my brothers and sisters. My stepdad had his own knife shop in Queens, and he spent many hours at work. My mom frequently spent the whole day in Brooklyn, traveling via bus, ferryboat, and train. She went there to spend time with her family and get a fresh supply of drugs.

My mom and my stepdad fought constantly, and sometimes they really went at it. They often argued over my mom's drug habit. I always sided with my mother, even when I knew she was wrong. As I grew older, I began to understand what the fights were really about: my stepfather was trying to get my mother to stop using drugs. He was trying his best to help her, and her drug use was really taking a toll on him. I didn't realize how special my stepdad was until I actually started writing this book and really thinking back on it.

I have blocked out so many things about my childhood from my mind through the years, and it's amazing to me that it all came back to me. Case in point: I remember sitting in the living room watching *The Six-Million-Dollar Man* on television. My mom was wigged out on her beloved drugs like always, so I was left to look after my siblings. My stepdad came home from work and asked where my mom was. I told him she was in the bedroom, sick. Whenever my mother was 'sick,' that was code for her being wigged out on drugs. I never made it a habit to look at my stepfather when he spoke to me, but this time I actually did. He had a this-is-it-I've-had-it look on his face, and he went into their bedroom and closed the door.

My first thought was that they were going to have another huge argument, but after five minutes of not hearing any yelling or screaming from their bedroom, I thought it all seemed really strange. To get to the bathroom in our house, we had to walk past their room, so I pretended I had to go to the bathroom so I could hear what they were saying. They were actually talking this time, not yelling or screaming. I couldn't hear what they were saying, but at least they weren't at each other's throats. It seemed Sam had decided to take a different approach with my mom. I found out years later that it was my stepdad that orchestrated a recovery intervention for my mother right at the house just days after that conversation. He got some of my mom's family and close friends from Brooklyn to come and stay with us while mom tried to quit her nasty drug habit.

At the time, I was about ten years old, and school had just ended for summer break. Everyone that was going to help with my mother's recovery was at the house. The first thing they did was search the house from top to bottom for drugs. They wanted to make sure she had zero access to any type of drugs whatsoever.

One of the people who helped out was a nurse; she got us all together to lay down some ground rules. The nurse informed us that an adult had to be with my mother at all times, even if she had to go to the bathroom. With what my mom was about to go through, they thought she may try to attempt suicide, so she had to be constantly supervised. She alerted us that my mom would be experiencing major mood swings and that some of her moods may be violent due to her body's reaction to withdrawing from drugs.

We were also informed that all of us kids had to stay away; we couldn't have any contact with our mother at all. Even though I don't recall the nurse explaining why those particular rules were set, thinking back, I completely understand now. The mood swings would be unpredictable, and they didn't want to take any chances in one of us kids getting hurt. They also knew my mother's mental and physical health would be in pretty bad shape. Her appearance alone would be frightening, especially to us. I believe that was the reason we had to keep our distance and have absolutely no contact with her. The nurse said the whole process would take between two to three weeks, and explained that my mother would be "quitting cold-turkey."

That first week was absolutely scary for all of us. Mom was in so much pain that she often yelled, screamed, and cried for hours on end. I remember flipping baseball cards in the living room with my brother one evening, and my mother came out of the bedroom. I will never forget it. She was trying to run, but she was too weak. She was dressed in pajama pants and one of my stepdad's white t-shirts. She was drenched with sweat, and her hair was a complete mess. My mother had such a desperate look on her face, like she was trying to escape from being tortured or something. I was frozen; I couldn't move a muscle. I couldn't believe what I was seeing. The caregivers immediately took her back into her room.

I ran right to my room, closed my door, and started to cry uncontrollably. Everyone in the house was warned about this in advance, but to actually see my mother in that condition was absolutely heartbreaking for me. I was on my bed with my knees tucked under my chin and my arms wrapped around my legs. I just kept rocking back and forth and saying, "Hang in there, Mommy. Hang in there, Mommy." Yeah, those first eight to ten days were pure hell for everyone!

After two weeks, my mom started to look like a new person; she didn't have that look of desperation on her face, her hair was combed, and most importantly, she was smiling her award-winning smile.

The people that helped my mom stayed with us for a total of three weeks. It was great to see my mother as a completely different person, like a huge bolder had been removed from her shoulders.

Before that, I had no idea my mother was skilled in arts and crafts. My stepfather signed her up to take art and ceramics classes a few blocks from our house. She certainly had skills. She did mostly oil canvas paintings of nature and farmhouses. She painted trees and the sky—all the things she wasn't accustomed to. She was in her own world when she painted, and she also made some very nice pieces in ceramics class.

Things at home were great after that. It seemed like I had more time to be a kid because my mother actually took over as far as running the house. She also kept busy painting portraits, crocheting blankets, and making ceramic pieces. Her trips to Brooklyn stopped completely, and she was more involved with us. She even organized a basketball tournament in the park for all the neighborhood kids, and I started inviting friends over to hang out at the house. It felt really good to hear my friends say, "Your mom's cool." And, man, I didn't realize how good of an athlete my mother was until she came outside to shoot hoops with us. She also challenged all the kids in the neighborhood to race her, and she beat each and every one of us by at least three steps. Yeah, life was pretty damn good at 43 Glenwood Avenue after my mother's intervention.

Things stayed that way for about four months. The best thing Mom did during those four months was to stay away from Brooklyn and her drug buddies. Then, she started taking trips back to Brooklyn again. Her trips became more frequent with each passing week. The next thing I knew, my mom and stepdad were arguing and fighting again. Mom was back to square one, using drugs again. For me and my siblings, it was like falling asleep and having a short-lived dream of a normal childhood, then waking back up to the nightmare that was our old life—our real life. Again, I had to spend most of my time babysitting while my mom traveled to Brooklyn to stock up on drugs.

When I wasn't grounded, I would shoot over to the park and play every chance I got. The more I played football with the neighborhood kids, the more I got into the sport. Before long, I started wanting to watch football on TV. I remember watching famed Chicago Bear Walter 'Sweetness' Payton, Number 34, and he became my idol. After watching Sweetness, I knew what position I wanted to play. I thought being a running back was the best position in the world, and whenever I went out to the park to play tackle football, I tried to run like Walter Payton.

People couldn't tackle me. In my mind, I was Sweetness reincarnate, even though I wasn't wearing a 34 on my shirt and being screamed at by Ditka. At the time, playing in that park was an important time for me, my moment in the sun. It became my release, my break time from the real world. The world I had to go home to every day consisted of watching my brothers and sisters, taking care of my 'sick' mom, and hearing and seeing the arguments and fights between her and my frustrated stepfather. Sometimes I found myself sitting on the edge of my bed, just wondering, hoping, and praying that things would change.

School began to get really difficult for me. I had a hard time concentrating, and my grades weren't very good. I was a D+/C- student at best. At the time, I had a lot of things on my mind and simply couldn't focus on school. It seemed like my teachers understood some of the things I was going through, though, and they made the transition much easier for me. I was pretty messed up mentally, and I believe that if it wasn't for my teachers at my elementary school, PS 35, there's no telling what could have happened. They never gave up on me.

My stepfather was a die-hard Jets fan, and he loved football, but in spite of this common interest that I could have shared with him, my brother took more to him than I did. I was considered a mama's boy in my stepfather's eyes because I never wanted to do anything with him. Little did he know the real reasons why I didn't want to be around him. My brother, Jemal, on the other hand, clicked with him from day one. He followed Sam around like a duckling after his mother duck. They formed a pretty close bond, and Sam took Jemal to Jets games and gave him rides to work.

It was different between us. I pretty much stayed away from my stepdad as much as I could and stayed close to my mother instead. When I wasn't with my mother and wasn't grounded or babysitting, I tried to go out and interact with the neighborhood kids and play as much as I could, although it didn't happen very often. Going out and playing team sports wasn't the norm for me; that wasn't my world.

My stepdad watched every Jets game that aired on television. I always wanted to watch the games, but I didn't want to watch football in the same room with him, and that was a problem because we only had one TV. I used to sit off to the side in the dining room and watch from there. I remember watching Joe Namath, Bruce Harper, Mark Gastineau, and Joe Klecko. I remember hearing my stepdad cheering them on, yelling and screaming at the television. He often asked me if I wanted to go to the games, but I always turned him down because I was still in that I-don't-want-to-be-around-you phase. He never really pushed and always just said, "Okay," before he'd grab my brother and head off to the game. I never really knew if I was hurting his feelings or not.

I remember my mother pulling me aside at one point. Mom never asked us anything; she just told us what to do. "The next time he asks you to go to a football game," she said, "you have to go with him." There was nothing I could do about it, and when he asked me to go to the next home game, I had to offer a reluctant, "Yeah, I'll go."

I remember that day because my stepfather had a routine prior to going to the game. We got up that morning, met up with his friends, and ate breakfast. Then we jumped on the train to Shea Stadium. We went to the concession stand and got the Game Day program, and then we took our seats to watch the players come out for pre-game warm-ups.

I really didn't say much during the whole process, come to think of it, but when we got inside that stadium, I was in awe. When I sat down in that seat, I was mesmerized, albeit still silent. When the players came out, I watched Bruce Harper and Joe Klecko warm up. When Joe Namath came out of the tunnel, the crowd went absolutely nuts! I was starstruck as I watched the professional athletes. Watching them on television was one thing, but seeing them up close like that was pretty amazing for me. I was about ten or eleven in the stands that day, and I decided right then and there that I wanted to play professional football. I wanted to come out of that tunnel just like Namath, and I wanted to look up and around and see all of those people. I just wanted to play. I never mentioned that to anybody at the time, but it was all I wanted to do. I wanted to be like Walter Payton, my own version of Sweetness.

After the game, of course, I downplayed that whole day. No one knew how much that day meant to me—no one! That game changed my life, though, and as much as I tried to hide it from everyone, now I actually had a goal. Before, all I wanted to do was just have enough time to go out there and play with my friends, but the thought of playing professionally hit me straight in the heart. After seeing those athletes play that day, I realized it was all I wanted to do, and I wanted it more than anything.

In spite of my high hopes and dreams of grandeur, I was smacked back to reality when I went back home. It was the same thing over and over again. With Mom heavy on drugs, I was stuck playing babysitter all the time. I guess you can say the real world gut punched me once again. Back then, my mom was extremely hard on me; at times, I felt she was even kind of mean to me. There were times I didn't think my mother actually liked me at all. I never understood her attitude toward me. Sometimes when she looked at me, it sent chills down my spine. Her looks on those occasions were so cold and hateful that I would have to look away.

I remember coming home from school one day and needing to use the bathroom. The first thing I did was run in the house, drop my books on the dining room table, and hurry to the bathroom. Not realizing that anyone was in there, I immediately opened up the door. What did I see? My mother was in there, shooting drugs up into her arm. I knew my mom took drugs, of course, but that was the first time I'd ever witnessed it firsthand. I was in total shock! I stood there for a few seconds in utter disbelief. For that brief moment, I think I was more embarrassed for her than I was for myself, but even as young as I was, that embarrassment quickly turned to anger. I looked at her and yelled, "Why do you keep doing that to yourself? Why do you do that?"

I started walking away, and she called me back. She said, "Come back here! Get in here."

I stared at her and walked in the bathroom. She told me to close the door, so I did. We only had one bathroom in the entire house, and that one bathroom was pretty small. When I closed that door, I realized I was only about two feet away from actually touching my mother while she had the needle in her arm, and that completely freaked me out. I remember leaning my body away from her while I made my way past her to sit on the toilet. I asked her, "Why am I even in here?"

She said, "I want you to see what I'm doing because I never want you to do this. Eventually, this is going to kill me, and this is something I never want you to do, so I want you to see what I'm doing."

I asked her again, "Why do you do it, Mom, if you know it's going to kill you? Why do you do it?"

She paused for a second with the needle still in her arm. I watched tears spill from her eyes and run down her face. She continued shooting up and said, "I have a story to tell you. I need to tell you something…" She proceeded to tell me about an event that occurred when she was eighteen years old. She said she was walking home after marching band practice after school, and two men grabbed her, covered her mouth, and dragged her into an apartment building. They took her all the way up to the roof where a third man was waiting. She said after that, the only thing she remembered were her clothes being ripped off and each one of those men taking turns molesting her, raping her. After they got done with her, they were about to throw her off the roof, but they thought they heard someone coming or else something distracted them, so they just hurriedly threw her to the ground and ran. "Three weeks later, I found out I was pregnant," she said.

She never mentioned to me that she had reported the incident or had an abortion, but she did say that attack was pivotal in her life, as it was because of that incident that she started taking drugs. The drugs took the pain away and kept her from having to think about what had happened. At the time when she told me this story,

I didn't really understand the implications, but as the months went by and the more I thought about it, it became obvious to me. Prior to that, I had always been told my biological father had died in jail, but now I presumed myself to be a product of a vicious gang rape. I never really put all the pieces together until I got a little bit older, but then I knew I was a product of the most tragic event my mom had ever gone through, and sometimes when she looked at me, she had to relive the nightmare. No wonder she had such mood and attitude swings toward me!

From the time my mom shared that horrible story with me, I felt sorry for her and became more protective of her. Anytime she got sick, I went into overkill mode and really tried to take care of her, even more so than I did before. I know it wasn't my fault in what happened to her, but for some reason, I felt guilt on my shoulders. I became more defensive on my mother's behalf when she and my stepfather got into arguments and fights. In fact, I didn't hesitate to jump in and say, "Don't talk to my mother like that!" It was something I'd never done before, but knowing what my mother had already been through changed how I felt about her.

My mother was pretty strict on all of us, but she was extremely strict on me because I was the oldest. I couldn't get away with anything. If I left one dish in the sink, I was grounded. If I accidently talked back, I would get a smack in the face and then get grounded too. I was put on punishment more times than any kid on the planet, or at least it felt like it.

As I was growing up, my interest in sports continued to blossom. My mom knew that, so she used it as a tool to make sure I did what I was supposed to do. She knew I loved going to the park and playing ball, so she made sure I first took care of business at home. I guess the message she was trying to give to me was that it is important to take care of your home life and your family first. I did not realize what she meant by that at the time, but looking back, I see that in spite of her problems, my mom was probably one of the most amazing people I ever had the opportunity to know. Yes, she did drugs, but she always made sure we had a roof over our heads, food in our mouths, and clothes on our backs. We were always taken care of first, before she went and did her thing.

I guess the greatest thing Mom ever did for me personally was giving birth to me. I don't think anyone would've faulted her for having an abortion under the circumstances, but she chose to give birth to me—to give me life. For me, that makes her the greatest individual on this Earth and the best mom I could ever ask for!

Back then, in the 1980s, professional wrestling was a big deal. I remember my siblings sitting on the living room floor with me watching WWF stars like Andre the Giant and Bob Backlund. All the neighborhood kids were big on wrestling too. Once, when I was in fifth grade, the kids in school were talking about wrestling moves. They often had wrestling matches after school in the sandbox because it was the closest thing we had to a 'squared circle.' When one of the kids challenged me to wrestle, I told him I couldn't because I had to go right home after school. As a result, I was taunted and called names, and it wasn't a very nice feeling. The insults kind of pissed me off, as fifth-grade boys tend to have their egos and 'manhood' easily bruised, so I finally agreed to meet him after the three-o'clock bell. At the end of the school day, there was already a huge crowd gathered around that sandbox, waiting for me to wrestle this kid. I don't think I will ever forget his name: John Desario. I don't know if he got out of school early or if he just cut class, but John's older brother was also there, even though he was either a middle schooler or a freshman in high school already and should have still been in class. My brother was there to cheer me on as well. I entered the sandbox and we were ready to rumble.

I remember hearing John's brother say, "Get that nigger off you!"

The remark flipped some kind of switch in me, and the next thing we all knew; I flipped him into the sand and put him into a full nelson. I start squeezing as hard as I could, asking him over and over again, "Do you give? Do you give?" I didn't want to hurt him, but I was pissed off. I kept asking him, demanding an answer.

Finally, he uttered a feeble "I give," and I released him and let him go. I stood over him and offered my hand. He grabbed it, and I pulled him up.

His brother started taunting him and calling him names. "I can't believe you lost to a nigger," he said. John just looked at me and walked off, and I turned away and went home. The next day at school, John came over to me and shook my hand and apologized not for the wrestling, but for what his brother was saying. After that, John Desario and I were very good friends.

By the time I reached junior high school, things had gotten worse in regards to the babysitting and watching my brothers and sisters. My mom's drug use was heavier than ever, making it diffi-cult—if not impossible—for me to go out and have a normal child-hood. Still, I was able to have some interaction with the neighbor-hood kids, and I had pretty good relationships with them. During that time, all of my friends began to call me 'VT,' and to this day, that is the name I go by with most people.

My brothers and sister. My baby sister, Ellen, was asleep.

Chapter 5:
Team Sports

Clove Lakes Park was the place where all the kids played. On Fridays and Saturdays, we played our version of tackle football. At the time, everyone except me was affiliated with a team in organized sports. On a daily basis, my friends would practically beg me to join their baseball, basketball, or football team. Everybody wanted some VT, but none of them knew my family situation, and I did not want them to know what I was going through at home. I just explained that I was too busy with too many things at home, and because of that, I really couldn't play on their teams.

One of the kids did convince me to play baseball for his church league. I had never played baseball before in my life. I told him I couldn't play in all the games, but that I would play whenever I could. I had a blast and ended up being one of the best players in the league. It was a lot of fun, but I wasn't able to attend all the games because of my situation at home.

Things really didn't change for me until one weekend when I met up with the guys at Clove Lakes Park to play football. There was a coach from one of the Pop Warner football teams, there to watch us play. I did not know until afterwards that one of the kids from his team had told him, "You need to come out and watch this guy play. We need him on our football team."

To make a long story short, after we finished playing that day, the football coach pulled me aside. His name was Bill Thatcher. He asked me my name and asked if I was interested in playing on his football team.

Again, I was too embarrassed to let him know about my home situation, so I brushed him off and said, "No. I have a lot going on at home, and I'm too busy, Coach. I just can't play." Walking away from him was probably one of the hardest things I ever had to do because I really wanted to play, and knew I was pretty good. I had already learned that football is perhaps the only sport you can play while you're pissed off and actually still do well. Whenever

I played football, I was able to let out all of my anger and frustration. I truly fell in love with the sport for that reason, as well as many others.

A couple days later, the doorbell rang at my home. It was Coach Thatcher. He asked if he could speak to my mother. At the time, my mother was home, but I was afraid to even let him speak to her. I tried to close the door while saying to him, "My mom's not home right now. Can you come back some other time?"

As I was rudely closing the door in the coach's face, my mom yelled in the background, "Who's at the door?" She came out from the back room, and though I didn't know what kind of condition she was in, I had no choice but to open the door. After the coach introduced himself, she invited him in and told me to leave the room. She thought he had come to the house to tell her about something I had done wrong, and she didn't want me to interrupt. I obeyed and went outside.

I remember staring through the window. I couldn't really hear what they were saying. I just saw them talking while I paced back and forth in the street. I remember the coach coming out with a straight face. I couldn't read him. I don't know what that coach said to my mother, but he somehow convinced her to let me play on his football team.

"Welcome to my football team," he announced to me. "I'll see you at practice tomorrow."

I shook the coach's hand and started smiling. I couldn't say anything because I was in total shock, so I just stood there with a huge cheesy grin on my face.

I remember that first practice very well. There were two guys I knew from playing in the park, but I didn't know the rest of the team. Of course, being where we were, I was the only Black guy on the football team, and they weren't too receptive of me, nor I to them!

The coach ordered all of us on the line to run a sixty-yard sprint. When they saw me jump out about fifteen yards in front of all the other kids, the coaches all looked at one another in amazement, and the next thing I knew, they were trying to give me the ball every chance they got.

Although I enjoyed playing for the football team, it was really difficult for me to keep my situation at home from the coach or anyone else. None of them knew I was babysitting all the time, taking care of my mother when she got sick, or breaking up fights between my mother and stepfather. The pressure was really getting to me. Even though she knew my practices were at five thirty every evening, Mom still insisted on taking her daily trip to Brooklyn as soon as I got home from school. Whenever she came back late (which was often), I had to dash out of the house, jump on the bus, and try to make it to practice on time.

The coaches didn't know what was going on, and the other players didn't know what my situation was. All they knew was that I was getting to practice far too late far too often, and I could see they were treating me differently as a result. The coaches got on me about getting to practice late, but since it was obvious I was the best player they had at the time, they still played me on Saturdays, even though it was against their policy to let the practice late-comers off the bench.

As irritating as it was for me and for them, there was nothing I could do about it. I was too embarrassed to talk to the coaches about the reasons behind it. I felt bad because they kept playing me, and my teammates saw how they were bending the rules for me and starting to resent me. I went to one of the practices (without my equipment) and told the coach, "I can't do this anymore. I can't play anymore. I've got other things going on at home, and I just can't do this."

Coach Thatcher tried to talk to me to see what was wrong. He asked me if there was anything he could do to help, but I told him there wasn't, and I went home.

Later on that evening, I was in the park, just goofing around with my friends. I don't know how that persistent coach found me, but when he did, he sat me down and said, "Whatever you're going through at home, I don't want you to quit." He told me to do whatever I had to do to make sure I made it to practice. He even offered, "If I have to pick you up, I will." He asked me, "Would it help if I moved practice to an hour later to give you a chance to make it on time?"

"Yeah," I said. "I guess it would help."

He told me to take down his number. "If you need me to come and pick you up, I will. I don't want you to quit. You're too good, and I know you love the game." He also encouraged me to use whatever I was going through at home to motivate myself. Coach Thatcher told me, "Go out on that football field and use that aggression. Get that stuff out of your system on the football field. Flip your switch, you know? You flip that switch. This football field is your salvation. This sport can really help you."

I promised him I wouldn't quit and that I would never forget that conversation he had with me. To this day, the flipping of the switch that he talked about has stuck with me, and I have always remembered to use aggression to my advantage. Those are the things that were taught to me at a very early age, and they enabled me to enjoy a very successful peewee football career. For two years, I played for Coach Thatcher's team and pretty much broke every record there was.

I did so well that I even drew the attention of some high schools. My last year in the peewee football league, I drew the attention of one called Poly Prep, a private school in Brooklyn. It was one of those schools that required a lot of money to attend, and the football coach offered me a scholarship. My mom did not approve. She didn't say so in so many words, but I knew she needed me at home to watch the kids so she could continue her drug-run commutes back and forth to Brooklyn. So, I had to turn down the scholarship to Poly Prep and ended up going to our local Curtis High School instead.

Age 12, sporting my Pop Warner football jersey.

Second Quarter

Chapter 6:
High School Beginnings

I was constantly reminded of my small size and stature, or lack thereof. In fact, off the football field, I was very self-conscious about it. Going into high school, I was only five-six and ninety-eight pounds. Not all of my friends were supportive of my aspirations to play football at the high school level. Everyone has a friend or two that are absolute haters, and those are the ones that wanted to discourage me; those are the ones that reminded me of my presumably inadequate size all too frequently when they should have been encouraging me instead. I didn't really need to be reminded, as I was all too well aware of it on my own.

I remember my first summer high school football practice. I was literally the smallest guy out there, extremely skinny, but I could run like a deer. Thank God He gave me the ability to run! At practice, I met a man named Fred Olivieri, who had recently taken over the head coaching position. Coach Olivieri had been an assistant for years, and it was only his second year as a varsity head football coach. The Curtis High School football team did not have a remarkable history, and they had not won a lot of games. In fact, I couldn't remember the last time I'd heard of them having a winning season.

I walked up to Coach Olivieri and introduced myself. He looked at me kind of strangely, probably because of my size. I told him I was trying out for the freshman football team. I shook his hand, he shook mine, and I went off about my business. As I was walking away, I thought to myself, *Man, that coach has a lot of hair on his lip!*

When it comes to playing sports—especially football—I turn into a completely different person. Off the football field, I was very self-conscious, always nervous about what people were saying or thinking, and always hard on myself. I hated making mistakes, especially on the football field. Whenever I could, I arrived at practice extremely early to get in some extra work. Thinking back, I was a different kind of kid; I was always hard on myself, my own worst enemy, so no one had to push me to get something done when it came to playing football. I noticed at a very early age that I was extremely passionate about playing the game of football. I absolutely hated making even the slightest error on the field, and I played the game with a lot of emotion. At times, I had tears running down my eyes while I played because I wanted so badly to score or make a tackle. I don't think I ever took anything more serious than being on that football field.

When I wasn't playing football, I never thought I did anything right, but on that field, I gained extreme confidence. At times, I played with bad intentions. There was a lot of anger and frustration built up inside of me. I literally turned into a different person on the field. I think if you would've checked my DNA as the person on the football field and the person that just walked around as a civilian; it would have come up different. There was a huge, noticeable difference in my attitude and demeanor once I put on those pads and cleats. Off the football field, I considered myself a caring person, kind of shy and reserved and definitely not as confident. But, when I put that helmet on and strapped it up, I became something else entirely.

I was so light that during my freshman year and the beginning of my sophomore one, I used to tie ten-pound weights around my waist because I thought I'd get cut from the team for being less than 100 pounds. I was so paranoid about my size. I remember the summer time, before my sophomore year, when I saved up what little money I had so I could buy protein drinks to help me gain weight.

I knew I was small, but I also knew I could play the game. All I wanted to do was show my stuff. My childhood dream was to be like Walter Payton, and to do that, I had to learn to be a damn good running back. Little did I know that the Man Upstairs had given me an additional ability besides running. I found out by accident that I had the God-given ability to actually throw a football.

It was at that very first practice that I figured this out. I went out for a pass, and the quarterback overthrew me. I ran to get the ball and threw it back to the quarterback, thinking nothing of it.

Incredibly, at the very next practice, I was informed that I would be trying out for quarterback, not running back. I was not happy about this decision for several reasons. First, I wanted to play my childhood hero's position, which was running back. Second, I wanted to wear his number (34). And third, I always thought quarterback was a sissy position and envisioned it being reserved for punk-asses who wanted to get all the glory and do little of the work. I thought, *How can a quarterback possibly let out his aggression?* As small as I was, I considered myself extremely physical, and I thought it would be virtually impossible for me to show my toughness by playing quarterback, so I really had a problem with the suggestion. I can recall asking the coach several times, "Are you sure you want me to play quarterback?"

The assistant coach informed me that Coach Olivieri wanted me to change my position to quarterback. Despite my disappointment, I was a competitor. If I was going to have to play the quarterback position, I wanted to be the best at it, so that's when my quarterback career started.

Going into my freshman year, I was focused on playing football and not much else. Football became the most favorite sport in the world for me. I forgot about boxing, and never mind wrestling. No other sport mattered, period. I felt I was pretty good at it, and I really wanted to play at a high level. At that point, football became my life.

One particular weekend while I was preparing for my first high school game, I got grounded for not doing a chore around the house. I desperately wanted to play in that game. I had never purposely disobeyed my mother before, as I would never dare to go against her wishes and always did whatever she told me to do. I got grounded on Tuesday; the game was on Saturday. That whole time, I was scheming on how I could get out and play, even though I knew I was grounded from it. Somehow, I convinced my mother to let me go out. "I just want to go to the park and meet my friends and hang out, Mom," I told her, and she bought it. Of course, the place I really went was right to that game.

During the second quarter, I looked over at the fence and, to my horror, saw my mother. If looks could kill, I wouldn't have made it to the third quarter. At halftime, I went right over to her. She said, "You finish that game. You go ahead and you finish that game and bring your ass right back home." She did not look happy, and I was afraid to go home, not knowing what would happen when I got there.

I was able to finish that game, but I didn't have such a good second half because all I could think about was my mother. When I got home, she was asleep; I think she had passed out. I don't know if she forgot about it or what, but it was never brought up again. I was fortunate enough to make it through the whole season, and I only missed two games due to being on punishment.

While my life on the field was going well, things were getting worse at home. My mom was still heavily using drugs. I was in care-giving mode more than ever: cleaning the house, taking care of my mom when she got sick, breaking up more and more fights between her and my stepfather. Everything just got worse, and I found I was needed more at home than ever before.

The one thing about my mother being so strict was that she ruled with fear. We were scared of our mother because we knew she did not play around. We never had to be scared wondering what our punishment would be because she always did exactly what she said. If she said, "If you act up in school one more time, I'm going to whip your ass right in front of your classmates," then that's exactly what she did. She was one of those mothers that would never allow her kids to act like fools in supermarkets or other public places. She had no problem taking a belt out (which she kept conveniently rolled up in her purse) and spanking us right in the middle of the grocery store aisle if she felt it necessary. That's the type of fear we had. The good thing was, we always knew exactly what to expect, and there was no gray area with our mother. It was all black or white, and we were black and blue if we got out of line.

Please don't get me wrong; my mother was never abusive to us. In that day and age, it wasn't uncommon to whip your kids' butts. Back then, kids were spanked at school and spanked again when we got home. It wasn't uncommon to get disciplined that way, and I never felt physically abused by my mother.

At that point in time, my mom wasn't doing very well, and I still wasn't getting along with my stepfather. I wasn't too receptive to him. Our relationship was a lot better, but it was nowhere near what it should have been. I was still reserved; I still had resentment toward him for arguing with my mother all the time, and I just refused to let myself get close to him.

My mom and I had a crazy relationship. As strict as she was with me, I always stayed loyal to her. I always had her back. There is still one thing that will haunt me until I'm six feet under—something I've never revealed to anyone until now. The times when I was grounded or punished or when Mom kept me away from doing what I loved to do, I often wished my mother dead. She began to need me a lot more at home, and I always wished she would die so I could go to practice. I wished she would die so I could go to the game. I remember her being so hard on me. At the time, I often thought, *Why can't I have a normal childhood? Why is this happening to me? I wish she would just die and get it over with.* I remember thinking that several times.

As I grew older, I became more vocal and more confrontational with my mom. I was still very respectful, because I knew better, but I tried to explain to her at times how much football meant to me. We got into arguments and disagreements about me being grounded. Football was becoming a part of me; I literally got sick to my stomach if I missed practices. It was obvious that as I got older, I became more dedicated to the game, and that caused more arguments between us. But whenever I got too carried away, I earned a hand across the face, and that would basically put me in check.

The end of my freshman year, I was informed by Coach Fred Olivieri that I would be moving up to varsity as a sophomore. I was excited and scared at the same time. I was excited because it meant I was a good enough ball player to be elevated to the varsity level, but I was scared because I still only weighed 120 pounds soaking wet with a brick in my pocket. I was really tripping out about my size.

I became pretty close with one of my teammates, James Jenkins. We were both freshmen preparing for our sophomore year. James was a wide receiver, a big guy. As a freshman, James was six feet tall and 190 pounds. I was a David to his Goliath, but we formed a really good bond, a really good relationship, and soon became best friends my freshman year. James was the only one I confided in regarding my situation at home and almost everything else; he knew exactly what I was going through. It was James who taught me how to complete a Rubik's cube, something I found to be a lot of fun. To this day, I always have a Rubik's cube with me—not the same one, of course—and I find solving it a great stress reliever. It was just one of the many things James brought into my life.

Chapter 7:
The Day My World Changed

It was the end of my freshman season and it was Christmas time. I remember my mom was in a sober mood, which was different. She was very calm and wasn't yelling at anybody or telling anyone what to do. She got up for Christmas and began making a late breakfast for everyone. I walked into the kitchen and wished her a Merry Christmas, and she said, "Merry Christmas, baby." She said it in such a tiresome way, and she gave me an elongated hug and kiss on the cheek. She was behaving in a way I'd never seen before. It's really hard to explain. The only analogy I can think of to describe my mom's demeanor that day would be watching a boxer that's getting his ass kicked all over the ring, taking every punch you can imagine, but he refuses to go down. Round after round, he's getting pounded, and you wonder how in the hell he's still standing. But then, it's that one round, and that fighter is looking across the ring, and his face is saying, "I can't take anymore." That's the look my mom had. At the time, I didn't quite know what to make of it.

My family celebrated that New Years together while my mom was under the weather, not feeling well at all. On January 25, I woke up, got my brothers and sisters up for school, made them breakfast, and jumped in the shower. I usually woke my mother up after getting out of the shower, so I went to do just that. This time, though, she wouldn't wake up. I tried again to wake her. She started moving her head from side to side, but she was extremely groggy. I tried several more times to wake my mom up, but I couldn't.

My stepdad was already at work, so I called him and said, "I can't wake Mom up!" He told me to call the ambulance and get her to the hospital and that he was on his way back home.

I immediately called 911 and explained to them that I couldn't wake my mother up. They came over immediately, and I waited outside the bedroom door as they went in to check on her. They placed my mother on some sort of wheelchair cart. It looked like she was only half conscious as they rolled her out. As I was looking at her, I had an ominous feeling that I would never see her alive again. I felt a cold chill as the paramedics rolled her past me. It was one of the worst feelings I've ever had. But when the doctors said she had pneumonia, I didn't really think much of it. I thought she would be fine. I was sure she had just gotten sick, a little worse than normal, but she would be okay. It was just pneumonia after all.

The day before, I had argued with my mom about going to off-season workouts. I wanted to go, but she was giving me a hard time about it, so we had a big argument. Then, the very next day, she got sick and wouldn't wake up.

I went back to school. I did a little workout after, and the only reason I was able to do that was because my Aunt Shirley (my mother's sister) came and stayed at the house while my mom was in the hospital. That freed me up after school to do what I wanted, and that's all I thought about. I was excited because I didn't have to go straight home.

Two days passed, and my mom was still in the hospital. On the third day, we all went to visit her. I walked into her room, and I couldn't even recognize her. She wore false teeth, and they were out. She was extremely pale, and she just did not look like my mother at all. That really woke me up. Seeing my mother in that condition, looking so weak and frail, I got scared. I couldn't get a straight answer from anyone—not the doctors, not my stepfather, no one. They just said she was still real sick with pneumonia and would have to stay in the hospital for a few more days. That's all they told me.

I left the hospital, but I couldn't get that image of my mother lying in that hospital bed out of my mind. The strange thing is, as bad as my mom looked in that hospital bed, I never thought for one second that she wouldn't make it. I had a really bad feeling when they wheeled her out of our house, but I never thought in a million years that she would die.

The next day, January 30, I went on to school. I did a workout with James Jenkins again afterwards, and we threw the football around on the field before going home. "Jay," I said, "let's swing by the house, change clothes, and then go hang out at the mall."

As we were walking down the street to my block, I noticed my stepfather's car in the driveway, which was odd for that time of the day because he was usually at work. I walked through the door and saw my aunt, my brother, Jemal, and my stepdad. I wondered instantly what was going on. My stepfather yelled, "Why didn't you come straight home?"

Just then, my brother stood up, looked at me, and said, "Mom died."

The only thing I remember after that was that I looked at everyone. I know my friend James was behind me, but all I remember is turning back toward the door and running out into the street. I don't know what happened after that because the next thing I remember was being in my bed. I really can't remember what happened between the time I ran out into the street and the time I woke up.

I wouldn't talk to anybody. I couldn't. I was numb, in total shock. I had always truly thought my mom would live forever. She dealt with so much, had endured so much, and made it through. I never thought in a million years that she would go out like that. It was really difficult for me to talk to anybody, and I withdrew from everyone. It took at least a couple of weeks before I started to come around.

I remember getting ready for the wake but not wanting to go. I remember all six of us walking in there. I was in the back, and my siblings and my stepdad were walking toward the coffin in the front. It was the first time I had ever seen my stepfather cry or show any type of emotion of that magnitude, and that really threw me. He walked up to the open casket, stared at her, and grabbed her hand. I just stared at him because it was something I had never seen before. The only side of him I had ever known was yelling and arguing with my mom all the time. I never knew until that moment that the man actually cared very deeply for my mother. I finally made my way to my mom; I got about two feet from her coffin and I just stopped, it didn't look nothing like my mother in that box. I couldn't believe that it was her laying there! It's extremely hard for me to describe my thoughts and feelings at that particular time... I was completely numb inside.

We made it through the wake, and the next day was the funeral. I remember going to the church and seeing them place the casket in a Hearse and everyone getting in their cars. The Hearse drove to the house. It stopped in front of our house one last time for my mom, and then it went to the cemetery. I remember going to the cemetery and placing the casket over the grave. They would not lower the casket until everyone was gone. Everyone started to leave to go back to their cars, and I just stood there in front of the casket, blaming myself because of all the times I had wished her dead whenever she grounded me and kept me from playing sports.

I honestly thought it was my fault my mom was dead. There at her graveside, I apologized to her for arguing with her before she died. The last words I heard from my mother were "You're grounded," and the last words I muttered under my breath were, "I just wish you would die already." That's something I'm going to have to take to my grave—something I will never forgive myself for. Because in that moment, right there in front of my mother's casket, I was reminded of the sacrifices she made for me and my siblings, especially the ultimate sacrifice she made when she was just eighteen years old. All of those things came to my mind. I can't really put into words how I felt right then and there, but one thing was certain: I was completely heartbroken.

Guilt and regret are two terms I'm probably going to carry with me for the rest of my life in regards to my mom. It was the worst day ever for me and my family. I did not realize until then that my mom was the nucleus of our family. She was an amazing woman, and she is even more amazing now in my eyes because I realize the sacrifices she made to provide us with the life that we had.

Hell, I thought I was already grown, but after my mom died, I had to really grow up because I had to play the role of both parents while my stepdad was working. There was no one else to stay with my brothers and sisters. My aunt (on my mom's side) volunteered to move in to help with the family. I don't know what happened, but my stepdad declined her offer and told her we would be okay and that we'd make it on our own, so she never moved in. Understandably, it was a really somber, quiet atmosphere around the home for days after the funeral. The day my mom died, my world changed.

My mom and dad.

Chapter 8:
From Stepfather to "Dad"

Afew months after the funeral, I came home one day after school and saw my stepdad's car in the driveway. I said to myself, "What in the world happened now?" I walked through the house, into the living room, and into the kitchen, and there he was sitting at the kitchen table. He had his elbows on the table and his head resting in his hands. I asked, "What's up? What's going on?"

He looked up at me with watery eyes and said, "It's a rough day for me. I just miss your mother."

I remember walking up to him and just putting my arms around him, saying, "We're going to be okay, Dad." All my siblings called him 'Dad,' but I had never made a habit of it unless my mother forced me to, which she did on rare occasions. But from that day on, he was Dad to me. He showed me a side I never knew existed in regards to my mother and to us. I had never realized the sacrifices he made as well. He took a lot of riff and almost suffered disownment from his side of the family when he took us in. I did not know the things Sam went through and the sacrifices he made to provide us with the home that he did. But, on that particular day, I realized that he really, really loved my mom and really loved us. I wrapped my arms around him and said, "We'll be okay, Dad. We'll be okay."

Our relationship grew instantly from there, and we had a good one from that point on. He was more supportive as far as my football endeavors. He went to all the games he could possibly go to. Being that he was an avid football fan, the Jets in particular, it wasn't too much to ask for him to go to my games and watch me play.

My sophomore year was a difficult one, but I had to refocus myself back to the real world. I was having an extremely hard time dealing with the loss of my mother, but my dad was really good about knowing what to say and when to say it. He was absolutely fantastic, and we just all pulled together overall.

As I look back now, thinking about my dad, he was a pretty interesting man. He was a full-fledged Italian. He was very loud and very vocal and just told it like it was. He never sugar-coated anything and kept it real at all times. If he didn't like something or someone, he said so. There was no subtlety in his game. Perhaps I got that from him, because I can be pretty blunt and pretty direct, as my friends and family would attest to. We lived in Staten Island, which was predominately Italian. To be perfectly honest, the area that we lived in wasn't too far from where some of the so-called 'mobsters' were staying. There were times I thought Dad was somehow connected or involved or knew people in organized crime.

This one particular incident that took place that made me wonder about what involvement my dad had on 'the other side.' I remember playing in the middle of the street with my friends one time when I was ten or eleven years old. One of the high school kids that lived right next door to us was driving his car up the street. He saw us in the street and increased his speed. I literally had to jump out of his way to keep from being hit. I ran into the house immediately.

I wasn't really feeling my stepdad then because I still had issues with him being White and moving me from the only home I knew back in Brooklyn. So, I went to my mom and yelled, "I'm sick of it! These people are trying to kill me here!" When she asked what happened, I said, "The guy... he tried to run me over again. That guy next door."

The next thing I knew, I heard rattling in the kitchen, like someone was shuffling through a silverware drawer. I remember my stepdad coming out with a big-ass butcher knife and heading outside. My mom immediately jumped on him. My stepdad was pretty stout, about five-eleven and at least 230, so he just carried my mom's little ass right outside on his back. He was yelling from the time he walked out that door to the time he went over to the next-door neighbors'. The neighbors were out in their yard at the time. All he said was, "You keep your f***ing kid away from my kids, or I'll f***ing kill you. And if I ever hear that your kid did anything to any one of my kids, I'll kill you!"

Mom just kept pushing him back toward the house. My jaw dropped. I could not believe my stepdad was sticking up for me the way he did or that he called me his kid. It was amazing! But what was even more amazing (or should I say more suspicious?) was what happened next. I don't know if they were already planning on moving, but within the next forty-eight hours, there was a 'For Sale' sign on that house.

I never saw those people again. It just made me wonder and question, even today, if my dad had some kind of connection. Besides raising my eyebrows a bit, that incident also showed how much he had our backs and how much he cared. I was still being a hard ass about it because I still had my issues with him, but I never forgot that.

As far as the other people in my house, my siblings and I had a pretty good relationship growing up. I'm the oldest of five. My brother Jemal is three and a half years younger than me, and man, he was something else. He was one of those kids that just had to be around his big brother. He wanted to go everywhere I went, no matter where I was going or what I was doing. "Where's Vernon?" he'd ask. "Where's V?" and he followed me around like a little lost puppy. Jemal was a major pain in the ass growing up, or at least that's how I saw it then. I didn't really appreciate how he was with me back then, but I appreciate it now. I didn't realize how much he cared about me and loved me until we got older, and back in the day—especially after our mom passed—he was stuck on me like white on rice. We nicknamed him 'Blockhead' because he was always doing stupid stuff like playing with matches near a furnace or running his bicycle into a tree and injuring his head. I'm not sure who actually gave him that nickname in the first place, but it has stuck with him to this day.

Then, there was my sister, Sharlene. Out of all of them, I guess I was closest to her. We really got along well. I don't know what it was, but we just clicked. She was next youngest to Jemal in age. As the years went on, I nicknamed her 'Jake' (and I will probably get a major tongue-lashing from her for mentioning that in this book).

I came home one day from school. She was sitting at the dining room table doing homework, and when she looked up at me, I said, "What's up, Jake?"

She looked at me and said, "What"?

I said, "I don't know. You just look like a Jake right now," and it stuck.

While I got along with both of them, my sister, Sharlene, and my brother, Jemal, fought like cats and dogs. They did not get along well at all and never agreed about anything. So, of course, when Jemal found out that I nicknamed her Jake, he ran with it because he knew she couldn't stand it. They fought nonstop. Fortunately, things are a lot better between them now, probably because they're adults.

Out of the five of my siblings, I would say my brother, Brian, was the black sheep of the family. He lived by his own rules and did his own thing. He was a cool little dude back then. Brian was one of those kids you would find in the park with his hands in his pocket, just walking and thinking. He never really got into mischief as he was growing up, and for the most part, he kept to himself. It didn't seem like he had a favorite sibling, but he did get along with my sister, Ellen, and they grew up pretty tight. Maybe it was because they looked exactly alike and were only a couple of years apart.

In fact, Sharlene and Brian were under a year apart in age. All three of them were pretty close, and all three were exposed to the drugs our mom was taking when they were born. Each one was affected in a different way by her drug abuse. My sister, Ellen, got the worst of it. She's an adult now, but it is obvious she took the brunt of the exposure. Ironically, she is perhaps the sweetest person you'd ever want to meet. She always smiling and, in my opinion, she has a heart the size of Texas. Other than that, they were physically able to do whatever they wanted to do. We were all healthy and safe. To this day, we all try to keep in touch via phone or Internet, but it was pretty tough after our mom passed because we were all extremely close to her. That tragedy really drew all of us even closer together as a family, as tragedies often will.

I remember having different discussions with my mother. My mom had her deep moments when she was alive. She would always tell me, "You always make sure you all stay together. All you have is each other. Don't let anything or anyone split the family apart." That lesson was welded right into my cranium, and when Mom died, all I thought about was making sure everybody stayed together. For the most part, it was working out.

Chapter 9:
A Little Support from Brooklyn

After my mom passed, I started spending a lot of time traveling back to Brooklyn; I still call it home. I spent time over the weekends with my cousins and aunties, and I started clinging to them more. I hardly did that when my mom was alive, but when she passed, I took that trip to Brooklyn every weekend, especially during my sophomore year.

I rode the bus to the ferry and then took a train to get there. I walked all the way down Fulton Street to my Aunt Mable's house. She was another amazing woman, and she treated me like I was one of her kids. She opened her door to my family—especially me—and every weekend, I became one of her kids.

One of my cousins that I look up to is Derrick. He played football at Boys and Girls High School, and I believe they won the city title. Derrick was a tailback and a fantastic athlete. I admired him tremendously then and still do. His nickname is 'Chill,' and I thought it was so cool that by the end of my sophomore year, I had my friends calling me Chill, and I carry that name to this day. I wanted to be just like my big cuz because he is a hell of a man. During my weekend visits, I watched him play football for a semi-pro team called the Brooklyn Jazz. I could not believe my eyes, seeing the way he was running. He was so quick and so fast! He was short, but his feet and legs were moving so doggone quick that my head was in a daze just watching him play.

At that time, the Jazz had a silky smooth quarterback that everyone called 'Breeze.' He was so cool—majorly cool. At the time, I was playing quarterback on my own team, so I watched Breeze and dissected every little move he made: the way he faked a handoff, did a play-action play, or dropped back. I don't think I've ever seen anybody play the position the way Breeze played it. He was a very cool, smooth, and suave kind of quarterback, and I wanted to emulate him if I could. I was a human sponge. I watched carefully as he faked a handoff and placed the ball behind his back and just sat there flat footed and no one knew he had the ball. It was so cool to watch. As I sat there watching Breeze and Chill (my cousin, Derrick), I was more into the sport and more into the game than ever before.

It was unbelievable therapy for me because I needed that part of my family; I needed to be around them. If it wasn't for them, I don't know what would've happened, to be honest. I don't know what state of mind I would've been in. They reached out to me when I needed them, and they came through for me. I really needed that time with my mother's side of the family.

Back in Staten Island, we had a routine where everyone was accountable and everyone did their part. My brother, Jemal, was a little older, so he started to babysit as well. My dad understood; he knew I needed to be around the other part of my family, so he encouraged me to go to Brooklyn and spend time with them—and I'm glad I did for my football and my spirit.

Chapter 10:
More than Just a High School Football Coach

I believe it was my sophomore year that I grew a special, unbelievable, unbreakable bond with my high school football coach, Fred Olivieri. He's probably one of the best human beings (next to my mother and father) that I've ever had the pleasure of having in my life.

Fred became a very special person to me. He took a special interest in me not only as an athlete, but also as a human being. He also took an interest in my family. We really didn't have much money back then. Anything I needed financially—even money for camp—he was always pushing in my pocket. It was a relationship that just grew and grew and is still growing to this day.

To this day, I call him and tell him how much I appreciate what he's done for me and my family. It all started, I believe, my sophomore year when he really took me under his wing and became my second dad. Out of all the negativity I heard in regards to my athletic future or my athletic ability, I can say without a doubt that he was always in my corner and always had something positive to say. He never, ever shot me down. I wondered why he always had that mentality and attitude with me.

I spoke to him about three weeks before working on this book. I called him just to see how he was doing. We always reminisce about the high school days and the things I used to do as far as my training workouts. He used to tease me about tying weights around my waist so I could be heavy when I weighed in. I asked him, "What was it that gave you such an interest in me back in the day?"

He said, "V, I've never seen an individual with a bigger heart, a bigger drive, and a bigger passion not only for the game, but for life itself."

If he had explained that to me back in the day, I would not have understood, but I'm older now, and I get it. I am the type of person that doesn't do anything halfway, and he had passion for everything he did, even when he was teaching his oceanography class.

Coach Olivieri doing what he does best: changing lives!

He made me want to put on a scuba suit and dive down to the bottom of the ocean and have a look around. Fred is one of those people that like things done a certain way; he would rather do things himself (his way) than have someone else do it their way. I always found him a little 'anal,' and he was extremely structured. Everyone gave him a hard time about the way he was, but the great thing about Fred is that there is never any BS with him. Everyone knows where they stand with him. He doesn't trust too many people, and he has always been a huge believer in loyalty. If Fred can count on you, there is nothing he wouldn't do for you! There are no in-betweens with him, and everyone either loves or hates him. As you can probably tell, I love him!

Back then, Fred drove a little old green, two-door car. I don't remember the type it was, but some of the other guys on the team went out of their way to bust his chops about it. Once, they lifted that little car up and put it on the sidewalk, and that aggravated him quite a bit. I couldn't help finding it a bit funny because he started threatening the suspects with running laps after practice if he caught them. But, hell, they did that so much during my junior and senior years that Fred started laughing about it as well. Fred always had time for me and still does, and I can honestly say he is the only person on Earth that has never let me down!!

Senior year at Curtis High School.

Chapter 11:
Building Up and Working it Out, Inside and Out

My sophomore season, I was five-six, probably 120 pounds. I worked extremely hard in the off-season, preparing myself for my second year of high school football. I was still kind of messed up mentally at times due to the death of my mom, and I dedicated my time, my energy, my workouts, and my games to her. I actually had a pretty solid sophomore year and even played as starting quarterback. I passed for over 1,000 yards and had a really good year. At the end of the season, I received All-Star honors and broke some high school records—and I thought that was pretty cool! (What kid wouldn't?)

Then came my junior year, and I had to put new goals in place and rededicate myself. The first thing I wanted to do was increase my size. My stature was still a major concern for me. In spite of my throwing heroics, I wanted to run the football. My sophomore year, they didn't have too many running plays for me as a quarterback because of my size, but I did have the ability to throw the football, so that's what I did—a lot!

At the start of my junior year, I still had a running back mentality but had to function in a quarterback position. If I wanted to have my cake and eat it too, I had to develop my body. I did all sorts of workouts and spent at least two hours in the weight room three times a week. I even drank a lot of protein drinks to increase my weight. The one thing I failed to realize until Coach Olivieri reminded me was that I was young and my body was still growing and developing. That year, just before my first game, I was five-seven, all beefed up to about 150 pounds from a lean 125. I was still banking on the fact that I was still growing, but I had every intention of helping the growing process along with the additional weight training regimens I undertook.

At home, my brother, Jemal, had gotten a little older and was taking on a little more responsibility, thank God. My brothers and sisters were all in school, and that enabled me to devote more time to football. In fact, we all pitched in and helped one another out.

James Jenkins and I worked out together year round. We ended up having a stellar junior year, and we both made All-Honors, Honorable Mention All-State, and All-Star in New York City. I passed for 1,000 yards again, and my friend and teammate, James, was an absolute beast. He was a big physical receiver with an uncanny ability to catch a football unlike anyone I've ever seen at that level. James made my job as a quarterback a lot easier, and that gave me better rushing performance. Coach Olivieri (who we came to call 'Coach O') put in additional running plays, and I believe that was because he knew I still wanted to be a running back. My amazing coach knew I was a very physical football player, and I made every attempt to show him that at practice. I actually started developing some good muscle mass, and Coach O finally let me show more of my running skills.

I was all business during my senior year of high school.

As I said, Curtis High School wasn't known for winning a bunch of ball games, but we sure did make a really good name for ourselves on Staten Island and in the state of New York. The 'Turner-to-Jenkins connection' became a common topic in local newspapers. Certainly, James and I didn't play those games alone, and I wouldn't be doing my other teammates any justice if I didn't mention them. One such player was wide receiver, Todd Turner, and it wasn't uncommon to hear: "Turner to Turner for the score!" from the local media and sportscasters. I ended up throwing a lot of touchdowns, but they wouldn't have been touchdowns if James Jenkins and Todd Turner didn't catch them. By the time my junior year ended, I had received All-Honors for the second year in a row.

Next, it was time to mentally and physically prepare for my senior year. My training regimens got a lot more intense, and I even began to do some off-the-wall stuff like setting my alarm clock for two a.m. just so I'd have time to either do push-ups or a few sets on the bench or even go out and run a couple of miles. I remember one particular time when I got up at about one thirty, and my dad was in the living room dozing off on the couch. I had on my workout clothes and was trying to leave quietly when he said, "V, where you going?"

"I'm going to get a couple of miles in. I've got to get a workout."

He looked at me and shook his head and just smiled. I smiled and winked at him and went on to get my workout in.

My theory in doing that back then was that I wanted to be at least one to two steps ahead of my opponent at all times. I wanted to be a step ahead of the game in every aspect. I could get an extra workout while my opponents slept, and that automatically put me a step ahead of them. It is something I continued throughout the rest of my football career. I always tried to outwork my opponent because I knew that if I mentally felt I had worked harder, then I mentally felt I would do better on the football field. It was somewhat of a 'Jedi mind trick' I played on myself, but it worked. I truly believed those actions, those training regimens, and that focused, determined way of thinking would help me play successfully on Saturdays—and it did.

By the beginning of my senior year, I was five-eight and weighed in at 165. I had a very muscular stature. Not only was I more physically stout, but my mental toughness was off the charts because of the things I had been through at home and because of the demanding workouts I had put myself through. I was most definitely prepared to do some damage on the field. I was on a mission; I had no intention of holding anything back. This was my last go-'round, perhaps my last year to ever competitively play the game that I loved.

When I arrived in camp, I made sure to let my actions speak for me, and they did. Coach O had no choice but to add in special running plays for me because I ran with a vengeance. I was a tail-back in a quarterback position. My idol was and always will be Walter 'Sweetness' Payton. And, if you know anything about that man and the way he played the game, you know he played it with all his heart. He played the game with ultimate passion and gave it everything he had. He was a defender with the ball in his hand. That's the way I wanted to play, and that's the way I did play. I can recall times when I would call out to would-be attackers, "Let's do it! Let's bang!" and I never shied away from a healthy hit. That is something I solely got from Walter Payton. I was always looking to give a hit as well as take one. I realized that when I played the game that way, it made my opponents think, *Damn, this guy is crazy. This is one crazy little dude!*

That was the style of play I tried to maintain, but it was extremely hard to do it continuously because of my smaller stature, but my heart didn't know any better. I tried to be a defender with the ball in my hand, just like Payton. I never shied away from hits, and the more I put myself out there like that, the more confident and comfortable my coach felt, and the more he allowed me to run.

I became Coach O's double threat. He started to realize I could burn our opponents as easily in the air as on the ground. In high school training camp, when Coach Olivieri saw me scrambling, he always blew the whistle so no one would hit me, and that infuriated me. I was such an intense ball player, and I was always working on my craft. Taking the hit was part of my craft that I wanted to work on. I wanted to be able to withstand a hit and keep running, and the only way to learn that was to get hit, but Coach O was reluctant to allow it. He thought of me as the quarterback, the nucleus of the team, and he didn't want me hurt. He needed me for the season, and he just wanted to protect me.

I wasn't thinking like Coach O. I just wanted to get physical, I wanted to prepare myself in every facet of the game—and a big part of my game was the ability to run. So, whenever the coach quick whistled me, I would literally yell at him, "Stop blowing that whistle and let me finish the play!"

The coach wouldn't dare say anything to me on the field out of respect because I was the senior and one of the captains. I led with a fierce, competitive nature that he wanted, but he still pulled me aside at the end of practice and explained to me in private why he always gave me the quick whistle. "I need you, Turner, and you are more important to this team than you realize," he said.

He was right, of course, though at the time, I really didn't understand and realize the type of passion I was bringing to the game
or to our team. I had a very strong work ethic, and I didn't realize how much of an impact it had on the rest of my teammates. It
was something I just didn't see, but Coach O saw it as something
they had never had before in our program: a leader that led by
example.

James Jenkins ('Jenks') wasn't as enthusiastic in working out
as I was. I had to almost pull Jenks out of his house, and once we
were there, I threw about 300 balls a workout session. It paid off.
In our senior year, we were unstoppable. Besides Jenks and me,
there was also John Roda, a little Italian kid with a heart the size
of Mount Rushmore. Roda was one of the toughest little guys I
have ever laid my eyes on; that cat was all heart! Robert Tally, a
silky smooth defensive back, was extremely intelligent and was
my backup, though he never really stepped on the field as a quarterback because I never missed a game. We also had guys like Glen
Nardiello and Sam Litrell, two linemen who started from their
freshman years and played all four years. They were unbelievable
athletes, complete beasts on the football field. I could go on and on
about the guys on that team. We were the Warriors, both on our
high school jerseys and at heart.

Hooking up with my boy, John Roda.

From what Coach O told me, my teammates got their work ethics and their energy from how I conducted myself, the way I carried myself, my work ethic, and my passion for the game. I didn't have great grades and barely passed academically, so I knew there wouldn't be any academic scholarships coming my way. Besides being what I loved, football was the ticket to my future, so I poured all of my focus and heart into it, and my teammates followed suit.

You come across a person or two in a lifetime that absolutely captures your interest and your heart in a special way. A young man named Jeff Burkey was one of these people for me—an instant 'hit' in my heart from day one! We were beginning spring practice in preparation for my senior season, and we had a crop of up-and-coming ninth graders there to participate. It was a time when upper classmen could view the incoming junior high talent, as well as haze and hassle them. During one of our drills, I noticed a little bitty kid in the pass catching line; I thought I was small as a freshman, but this kid was only about five-four, weighing in at a meager ninety pounds wearing all of his clothes and probably his shoes, too. I don't think it was his stature that captured my attention so much as his demeanor and his smile that won me over. Jeff Burkey didn't say much of anything to anyone; he just smiled a lot.

The upper classmen didn't seem to give the guy any credit for trying, and in our first practice, they made so much fun of him for dropping passes. I couldn't blame him, though, considering the ball was bigger than he was! The older guys also teased him about his afro (a rarity on a White kid), his widow's peak hairstyle, and his eyebrows that seemed to connect into one long unibrow. Within ten minutes of that first practice, Jeff was dubbed 'Eddie Munster,' named after the creepy kid on the sixties sitcom. They really gave the little guy a hard time, and any other kid would probably have run home in tears, but not Jeff. No, Jeff just kept flashing his smile at everyone, the type of smile that revealed his personality and character—and it was that brave smile that intrigued me. Within forty minutes of that very same practice, I had decided I would be Jeff's protector. No one—and I mean no one—was allowed to pick on Jeff when I was around, and they knew better than to do it when I wasn't around either. By the end of the summer, Jeff was a part of my family, spending more time at my house than his own. To this day, I introduce Jeff to others as my brother. Oh, and did I mention that today, Jeff is six-three and over 200 pounds?

Jeff Burkey showing off his new ride.

I wanted to go to college, to play at that next level. So, in my senior year, I worked the hardest I ever had. I don't think I've ever been more focused, and by the time I finished my senior year, I broke all the passing records on Staten Island. I even won the Fugazzi Award, a very prestigious award given annually to the best football player on Staten Island. Through football, I was able to position myself to potentially select any college I wanted.

James Jenkins broke all the receiving records on Staten Island, so together, thriving off of each other's competence; we had a very productive senior year. In addition to his record breaking, Jenks was by far a better student than I was. He had over a 3.0 grade point average, an excellent student. He was also six-three and a massive 225 pounds. He had the grades, stats, and size, so James was pretty much set and had the pick of the litter when it came to what school he would go to.

I, on the other hand, barely had the grades to make it, so my selection wasn't as big. I remember getting a call from one of my assistant coaches. He asked me to meet him in the park; he wanted to talk to me about my future. He felt he needed to be brutally honest with me regarding my athletic career. He told me I really needed to focus on my grades, and he explained that while Jenks was a given to play college and perhaps pro ball, things for me might be a different story. He warned me that even if I was fortunate enough to get an athletic scholarship, I should focus more on getting my degree than playing beyond college football because the likelihood of my playing at the highest level was extremely slim.

Looking back now, I see what he was trying to do for me. He wanted me to have a long-term success plan, and in his opinion, playing anything beyond college was not going to be an option for me. He wanted me to have a fallback plan, and for that, I appreciate what he tried to do. But at age eighteen, focused only on my football goals and bull-headed as all get out, I didn't want to hear it. I took that conversation negatively and felt like he had more faith in James than he had in me. I translated his advice as saying that James was going to go pro, while I didn't have a shot in hell. So, what did I do about it? I got pissed and went into I'll-show-you mode. As I got older, I realized that my coach was just trying to look out for me that day, but at that particular time.

I didn't see it that way. Throughout my lifetime, that conversation has occasionally popped into my head, and I've used it as motivation. To be honest, it actually came in handy. In spite of all the unknowns and the questions about my future potential and long-term plans, one thing I did know was that I wanted to play running back. I was a quarterback during my entire high school career, so I had to make a decision. The only way I was going to play running back was going to be at a small school. I had opportunities to go to bigger schools like East Carolina or Temple, but they wanted me to play wide receiver or defensive back. None of them wanted me to play quarterback, of course, and I wanted to play running back. So, after talks with Coach O, whose advice I trusted infinitely, I made the decision to find the best small college football program in the country.

Chapter 12:
The Bo Jackson Story (Part 1)

One of my most memorable stories took place at the end of my senior year. As I mentioned before, I received every award you can think of at the high school level. One special award I received that year was called the Junior Heisman Award, given to the top players in the state of New York. That particular year, Bo Jackson presented the awards to the athletes because he was the actual Heisman award winner that year. Bo brought his Heisman trophy with him, and that's something I'll never forget. As he was talking and we were sitting at our table, I couldn't take my eyes off that trophy. I simply had to touch it, and I even tried to pick it up, but it weighed about fifty pounds. I was star struck, not as much by Bo as his trophy.

Bo was pretty impressive as well though. He gave a tremendously inspiring speech and talked about his disability, a speech impediment. He said he had to work extremely hard because he used to stutter all the time. It was something he had to bust his butt and work past. In that speech, I couldn't even tell he had a speech problem, but that was because of all the hard work he put into overcoming it. As a young athlete, I couldn't help but hang on every word Bo said because I wanted to be at that level and beyond.

When he got done with his speech and the actual ceremony was over, Bo sat at a table to sign autographs and meet the younger athletes. As you might imagine, there was a very long line. Coach Olivieri pulled me out of my chair and said, "Let's go. I want to meet him," but to be honest, he didn't have to pull me anywhere. I really wanted to meet him, too, but I tried to play it cool. I had seen him play on television, so I was pretty star struck with him as well.

Everyone else had something in their hand for Bo to sign: footballs, jerseys, football cards, and so on. I didn't have anything. I walked up to him, and he asked, "Hey, how you doing?" and shook my hand.

"My name is Vernon Turner," I said, probably sounding more nervous than I realized. I told him what position I played.

"Do you have something for me to sign? Need me to get you anything?" Bo asked.

I said, "No. All I want to do is shake your hand." I shook his hand, and he pulled away from me, but I held on and just kept shaking his hand. "I'll be playing with you or against you one of these days, so this is all I need."

Bo smiled and said, "Best of luck, son... and work hard. Hard work will pay off."

After that, I walked away and headed back to my table to pick up my award.

Coach O asked, "What are you doing?"

"I told him I didn't need anything signed."

"Are you crazy? That's Bo Jackson! We're at least going to get a picture with him." They had photographers there with Polaroids, so we took a picture with Bo, and he ended up signing it, which I thought was great. As amazing as that day was for me, and as confident as I was when I told him so, little did I know Bo Jackson and I would really cross paths again.

VT, Bo, and Coach O at the Junior Heisman awards, senior year.

Chapter 13:
My One-Season Track Career

If I had a chance to turn back the clock and change any part of my athletic career in high school, I would have run track for more than one year. I was so consumed with football, and I didn't realize until it was too late that my track workouts would've helped me in football that much more. To be honest, my thought process was kind of jacked up. I was so paranoid about my weight, and I thought if I ran for the track team, I would lose weight I couldn't afford to lose. I only ran my senior year, and I must say I had a blast. It was either Bob Andrews's first or second year as track coach when I ran for Curtis High School. There were a few things I really liked about Coach Andrews. First, he was able to outrun all of his runners; he was amazing. Second, he was just as competitive as me, perhaps even more so. I didn't realize how competitive he was until I participated in the Staten Island Championship Meet. I had already won the 100-meter finals; I was last in the rotation to go in the long jump. I had fouled twice, and Coach Andrews was so cool about it.

He knew I only had one more jump to qualify, but he was cooler than a fan. I remember walking over to him, smiling, and giving him a fist-bump. The best jump at the time was twenty-one feet, seven inches. I went over to the approach line, and I could see Coach Andrews pacing back and forth at the other end of the sandbox. "Eye of the Tiger" was rolling through my head, making me feel heroic like Rocky Balboa. I took three deep breaths and took off. I made sure to plant at least five inches from the board just so I wouldn't foul again. As I launched into the air, all I could think about was Carl Lewis's form, and it worked. My last and final jump was twenty-three feet, nine and three-quarter inches, and I broke a city record. I think Coach Andrews was the actual inventor of the Tiger Woods fist-pump, even though Coach was actually doing it with both arms in midair. It was a sight to see.

The third and perhaps the most important thing I liked about my track coach was that he was an overall great guy.

I ran the 100- and 200-meters, and I also participated in the long jump and the triple jump. During that time, Carl Lewis was the hottest thing in the track world; the man had the best form I had ever seen. I used to watch video clips of him running and doing the long jump. He was absolutely incredible. Coach Andrews gave me some touching compliments after our last track meet. He thanked me for being the ideal team player and went on to say that I was an absolute pleasure to coach and would be successful in anything I did. I was truly at a loss for words; I'm so hard on myself that I was never able to appreciate what he was saying to me then, but I appreciate it now.

I'm leading the pack at my high school track meet.

Chapter 14:
Carson-Newman, Here I Come!

Coach Olivieri conducted all the research in finding the 'ideal' college for me. I didn't find out until many years later that Coach O had spent hours on end calling schools and sending letters and highlight tapes; it almost became an obsession for him. Out of all the schools he looked into, one school stuck out like a sore thumb (in a good way). My decision to go to Carson-Newman College was because of Ken Sparks. I remember that recruiting trip like it was yesterday. I knew I was going to Tennessee, pretty far from home—about a twelve-hour drive from New York. Coach Olivieri really did his homework in researching that school. All the information we pulled up on the Internet was impressive. Academically, it was a top-rated school, and it had one of the best small college football programs in the country. They even had eleven different combinations of uniforms, and Carson-Newman just won football games. Oh, and I couldn't overlook the fact that they ran the ball 85 percent of the time.

The recruiting trip was pretty interesting. I flew out there, and one of the assistant coaches picked me up from the airport. It was in the afternoon, and it was close to getting dark. We had about a thirty-minute drive from Alcoa Airport to Jefferson City, Tennessee. When I got on the campus, we went over to the Athletic Coaching Office and met some of the coaches. Ken Sparks wasn't there at the time, most likely busy in a meeting.

I was sent over to the dorms to meet some of the players, and I wasn't impressed at all. I knew the school was small, but it seemed way smaller than what I had imagined. The dorms were dreary and cramped. To be perfectly honest, I really wasn't feeling the school at all.

I met a couple of the ball players. One of the guys I met was named Edwin Lowery. He was a 'red-shirt' freshman quarterback, meaning he didn't play at all during his actual freshman year and that he still had four years of eligibility to play. So, he was still a freshman, but that was his second year. Edwin had a lot of energy, and it was clear that he loved God. He had crosses all over the place and was a bit of a neat freak; everything was in order in his room. He was a very friendly guy. 'Easy-E' (that's what they called him) was from Florida—Pensacola, if I remember correctly. At first, I thought he took drugs. I was convinced he was on uppers because he was constantly bursting with energy.

Edwin was the one that showed me around and introduced me to the other ball players. We clicked just like that because I could tell he was genuine. Though he was hyper and extra friendly, he was honest, the real thing. The fact that he was Black only put me more at ease.

Even after he showed me around the campus, I still wasn't really impressed. I thought it was dreary and small, and nothing really caught my eye. I said to myself, "There is no way I'm going to sign at this place. No way." I met most of the players, and they were cool, but my mind was already elsewhere.

I wanted to get the hell out of there and take the next plane back to New York. But they saved the best for last, because one of the coaches came to the dorm and picked me up and said, "Okay, time to meet Coach Sparks."

Coach Ken Sparks was a living legend; as far as anyone at Carson-Newman was concerned, the man could walk on water. I went in his office and sat down. He asked me how I was doing and how my family was. He started talking about his faith, his belief in God. "It doesn't matter who we play or where we go," he said. "We're always going to put God first. It's amazing the power you have when you have Him in your heart. You can run through walls."

Honestly, as a New Yorker, I didn't want to be preached to by some coach from Tennessee, but the way this man was talking to me; he had my undivided, complete attention.

Coach Sparks told me they never mentioned the opponent's name while preparing for games. He explained to me that regardless of who they played, they did everything in their power to prepare themselves mentally and physically. "We have our faith in God," he said. "We leave it out on the field every time, and all the other stuff will take care of itself." He said, "You know, Vernon, we run about maybe eight plays at the most... well, twelve plays if you include run and pass. But those twelve plays, we run to perfection. You're going to get sick and tired of running the same old plays over and over again. We're going to put out different scenarios. We're going to put extra defenders on the field, and sometimes we'll play twelve against eleven. We'll play thirteen against eleven, and we'll run the same plays over and over again. Then, when we get out on that field for game day, all you are going to do is go out there and have fun. The most important thing I want you to do is to get everything you can possibly get out of the four years that you're here. First an education, then your belief in God, and finally, a fantastic athletic career."

Coach Sparks told me he knew about my work ethic and my work habits and that I was a perfect fit for the school. "You will be a leader by the things you do," he said. "I don't need to hear what you have to say most of the time. I want to see what you have to say." He told me I should go in there with the same mentality I had back in high school, the same toughness. Again, it was reiterated how tough I was, and it was good to hear it. He said, "I don't know if I've seen a tougher player than you, at your size," and he told me I was going to get bigger, faster, and stronger. He also told me he was excited about seeing me at my best.

By the time the illustrious Coach Ken Sparks got done with me, I couldn't think of any other place I would rather be than Carson-Newman College. He almost had me at hello. That's how powerful Coach Ken Sparks was, and that's how much of an influence he had on me, right from the get-go. Small dorms or not, twelve hours from home or not, I was hooked.

Third Quarter

Signing on with Carson-Newman College
with Coach Dennis Webb by my side.

Chapter 15:
My First Set of Wheels

The Fugazzi Award was a pretty nice honor that I received, an award given to the top athlete on Staten Island. The cool thing about this award was that we were given a $1,000 check, which really came in handy. Like any high school senior without a good set of wheels (or any set of wheels, for that matter), the first thing I thought about was getting a vehicle.

I went used-car shopping in the newspaper classifieds and finally found an old Big Bird yellow Volkswagen Rabbit. The lady that was selling the car was asking $700, but I got it for $500, so I thought I was getting a deal. I took a buddy of mine out to help me drive the car back. One thing I failed to do was inform my dad that I was getting the Volkswagen. When he got home and I showed it to him, he wasn't a happy camper.

My dad and I really got into it about that car! He wanted me to save the money toward college so I would have some spending money, but I thought I needed a vehicle. I was a senior in high school, and it felt like everyone except me had a car. My dad wouldn't let me use his car because it was his only means of transportation, and if I got into an accident or a wreck for whatever reason, he wouldn't have had a vehicle to use. I thought getting my own car would help, but I didn't think about the insurance and all the other responsibilities vehicle ownership entails. Dad refused to put me under his insurance, so, for the longest time that summer, while getting ready for college, I was driving around with no insurance, which was stupid and risky. That was the first and only time Dad and I had argued about anything since my mom died. It was a pretty heated argument, and we didn't speak for a couple of weeks. It turned out to be a pretty tough time for the both of us because we were both stubborn, and neither one of us would give in.

During the summer, just before heading off to college, things became pretty hectic for me. I started a vigorous training regimen, which consisted of a five-a.m. run around the neighborhood and weightlifting in the afternoon, plus agility and pass catching drills. I did that three times a week. I was preparing to do battle my freshman year at Carson-Newman, all while still handling my responsibility of taking care of my brothers and sisters. I even managed to pick up a part-time job at McDonalds. As a family, we kept it together, and everybody was okay under the circumstances. It was a pretty tough time because my dad was still upset with me about the car he didn't want me to have, and I was just as stubborn about keeping it. I told him I would take care of the car myself, and that's why I started flipping burgers and asking, "Do you want fries with that?"

About two weeks before I had to fly out to Tennessee for school, Dad and I got into it again about the car, particularly about me driving it without insurance. I said, "Well, will you help with the insurance?" and of course, he refused. He just didn't want me to have that car, and he wanted me to get rid of it before I went off to college. My intention was to park it in Staten Island so that anytime I came home from school; I would have something to drive.

So, once again we stopped speaking, and the two-way silent treatment lasted until two days before I was to fly out for college. I had planned a going-away party at the house. I invited all my friends, my coaches, and everyone to come out to wish me well. I told my dad about the get-together, and he didn't say anything. I reassured him that everyone would stay in the back yard and nobody would be in the house. He still didn't say anything when I told him about it. He just nodded his head, and that told me everything was cool.

The party came, and I had a bigger turnout than I expected. All of my coaches, friends, and even some of the neighbors showed up to wish me good luck. Everybody was having a good time as the music played, but my dad was sitting inside. It was a weekend, so he was off work, but he refused to come out. I think he felt like he would be intruding. Since we had been arguing, he didn't think I would want him out there. Finally, I went inside the house and said, "Come on, Dad! Come outside. The coaches are asking about you. Come out and have a good time."

He didn't say anything, so I just walked back out. About four or five minutes later, he came outside and started interacting with the coaches. It seemed like he was having a good time. That made me feel pretty good, but things still weren't right between us. We weren't in the best of moods with one another, and that car was still causing problems.

The next day, I packed all day to get ready for my trip the following day. My dad and I really didn't say much to one another. My brothers and sisters were giving me a hard time, of course. My baby sister, Ellen, put a little stuffed dog in my bag. I named it 'Ted' and took it with me everywhere I went. I carried Ted for years, until I lost him only about four years ago.

The next morning when I got up, I already had my bags placed near the door. Coach O had arranged to pick me up and take me to the airport. My dad was lying on the couch, sleeping, and I had to walk past the dining room and the living room to go out the front door.

I heard the doorbell ring, and I knew my coach was there to pick me up. I was still a little bit pissed off at my dad. I just stared at him as I walked past, and for some reason, I had the same odd feeling I once had with my mom—like I wasn't ever going to see him again. I reached over to him and kissed him on his forehead and squeezed his arm to wake him up and let him know I was heading out.

He woke up and told me, "Make sure you call when you get on the other side. I want to make sure you got there okay."

I said, "Okay, Dad," and kissed him again on the forehead. It was a weird, eerie feeling, and I hoped it didn't turn out like things had with my mom.

Chapter 16:
More Major Adjustments

My freshman year was probably the most difficult of all my four years of college, just as it probably was for many of you. There I was, a New York kid from a very fast-paced city, heading to the South, to Jefferson City, Tennessee.

The Southern hospitality was something I was not accustomed to. Hell, it didn't mesh with me at all. I did not understand it, nor could I comprehend it. It took me quite a while to get used to that Southern mentality. What was really hard for me was that Carson-Newman was predominately White. I knew that before going there, but to actually be right in the middle of it was a completely different story. The only minorities in the school were either foreign exchange students or athletes.

The other issue for me was that in New York, you never spoke to anyone you didn't know. No one talked to strangers because it might have started a fight. Things were different in Tennessee, and one of the more difficult things for me to get used to was when total strangers came up and spoke to me.

I remember when I wanted to open a checking account there. I went over to the teller at the front and told her I wanted to open up a checking account. She sent me to one of the offices, and the bank employee that worked with me was so very, very talkative that I became paranoid. I thought they were using some angle to steal my money or scam me into something. They asked me what seemed like too many questions. I bit my tongue and didn't say much. I was very vague and spoke very little because I didn't know what they were trying to do, but in the end, I had opened my first checking account.

Later on that day, I wanted to take some money out, so I went back to that bank. I said to the teller, "I want to take out $50."

She said, "Hi. How are you? What is your name? Don't you go to Carson-Newman? How's your family?"

It was obvious that everyone knew that the minorities that went to Carson-Newman were only there for one of two reasons. She put two and two together and figured out I was one of the athletes.

Again, she was asking me too many questions, and I guess I just snapped. I responded, "Lady, I just want my money. I just want my money. I don't want to talk, okay? I just want my money!"

Evidently, I offended her pretty badly, because she called the Athletic Department and informed them of my rudeness. That afternoon, when I arrived at practice, I was pulled to the side, and my running back coach, Dennis Webb, sat me down to have a talk with me. The way he handled it was really cool. He knew I was from New York, and he knew the mentality of New Yorkers. He also knew my background and the adjustments I had to go through. He informed me, "Not everybody has an agenda, Vernon, especially down here in the South. Here, everybody is just nice. They're just generally concerned, you know? They show concern, and they're just very nice, that's all."

At first, I wondered how in the hell he found out about what happened at the bank, and I got defensive about it and told him, "I don't even know these people and they're trying to get up in my business." I told the coach I appreciated what he was saying to me, but that it was going to take me a while, and I wasn't going to change overnight. "But, I will try to think before I speak. I promise you that," I swore to him.

"That's all I can ask for. Just know that nobody is after you and nobody has an agenda. They are just very polite here, so don't take it personal."

It took me every bit of two years to get accustomed to the Southern hospitality, and at first, I wasn't feeling it at all. The more people I met, the nosier they got—or at least it seemed like it. It took me a while to get use to that. One of the other difficult things in Tennessee was that I had only managed to build my body up to a solid 168 pounds. At the collegiate level, that is still extremely small to be a running back. People automatically underestimated me based on how small I was. So, I had to prove myself quickly, right from the time I stepped on the football field. I had to show them I meant business.

At the first practice, they had a kick-off return drill. We had to stay within the thirty yards sideline to sideline instead of the full fifty-three yards. There were five guys on kickoff and six guys on the kickoff return. They would kick the ball off, and the kick-off guys would run down. It was all freshmen, none of the upper classmen. I guess they wanted to see who was tough, who was fast, and who got after it—and I wanted to be one of them.

That was the time when I think I actually proved my toughness. I flipped the switch and went from the quiet guy off the field to a completely different person. I was extremely confident on the field, borderline cocky. I sometimes played with bad intentions and a chip on my shoulder. I played extremely pissed off most of the time, and that was my demeanor.

I never realized how small I was, to be perfectly honest with you, because I never played my actual weight. I always played a good forty to fifty pounds heavier than I was, even after I stopped strapping on weights. When I played, I purposely thought of myself as a big man and tried to play that way. During that drill, I did everything you could think of, from attempting to run people over with the ball to alluding people to stiff arms to showing the speed. I basically showed them I could play the game. That was the reason I was awarded a full scholarship. That first practice with Carson-Neman was my testimony of what was to come. I held my own during training camp. We had a freshmen team, but I went right onto varsity and was competing.

In fact, I was competing for a starting spot. Our starting tailback at the time was Kenny Tyson. He was All-World over at Carson-Newman, and he broke every record imaginable. He got injured and was out for the year.

Carson-Newman was a split-back option offense football team, which means they could have two tailbacks in the back field at the same time, and we pretty much just ran a run-style offense. We had a total of maybe ten to twelve plays for the whole four years

I was there, but we ran those ten to twelve plays to perfection, just like Coach Sparks had told me was expected. Everyone—our opponents included—knew what was coming, but they could not stop it. We focused on precision, speed, and consistency. During training camp, there were times when we ran the same play fifty times at practice. Hell, we ran it so many times that we could run it with our eyes closed. From the blocking assignment, reading the tackle-down block, the guards tackle-down block, to reading the defensive end, it was embedded in our heads what we needed to be looking for in that split second.

It wasn't a hard offense to learn, but we all had to be on point. We had to have the skills. We could not be slow and play on that offense, and speed was a requirement. That's what we thrived on. All of our backs and quarterbacks were fast. I think it was the second or third game of the season when I earned the starting tailback spot as a freshman. I was doing extremely well to make starting tailback at the college level, and I was really happy about it. I called home and told my dad and Coach O that I'd be starting tailback for the Carson-Newman Eagles. It pretty exciting news for me and for them.

Dennis Webb was our running backs coach, and he was probably one of the most genuine men I've ever had the pleasure of meeting. Anytime I had an issue, I went to him. Coach Webb was the first one that actually took me fishing. I had seen it on TV but never experienced it myself. It was funny because I refused to touch the worms, so he had to bait my hook for me. During our fishing trip, we sat there and just talked and talked. I talked about my background and many other things, and I told him about what I was going through with my family. He talked about his family and how he got into coaching. We sat there every bit of four hours. I ended up catching a little guppy and throwing it back into the water, but the fishing part of it was more therapy for me—just sitting and talking with a coach who became a friend of mine that day. Out of all the people in Tennessee, Coach Dennis Webb was the one guy I came to trust and rely on. He's a really good man, and he pushed me hard. I guess if you have a favorite, you are harder on them, because he would not let up on me. He wanted me to be the best. Evidently, he saw something in me, because he stayed on me, and I ended up becoming a starting tailback for him.

About three to four weeks into the season, I was putting up some pretty good stats as a freshman and doing extremely well. My family was also doing well back home. Dad sent me money every week to make sure I had something in my pocket. I even received a phone call from him, which was odd because I was usually the one to call him on the weekends to tell him about my games. It was the middle of the week. He called to ask me how I was doing and how my grades were. He told me my brother got a hold of my car and wrecked it. I had left my keys there at the house. Dad said, "I beat his ass about it, but I'll tell you what... he took it out to Silver Lake. He and James went joyriding and hit a pole."

My brother was fifteen years old at the time and James was his best friend. Apparently, they were able to drive the car back to the house and park it. My sister ratted on him. I was upset about it, but I asked if my brother was alright and realized I couldn't do anything about the car from where I was, and it was too late anyway. Deep down inside, I think my dad was happy about it because he didn't want me to have the car in the first place, and now I would have to get rid of it.

Chapter 17:
The Day My World Changed... Again

I think it was maybe my fifth or sixth game of the season at a home game. We had just won, and I had a pretty good game. When I went back to the dorm room and called my brother to tell him about the game, he told me Dad had a stroke. He didn't know how bad it was; all he knew was that Dad was in the hospital. Apparently when he was unlocking the doors at work that morning, he just collapsed. My Auntie Shirley came to the house to stay with my brothers and sisters. My brother told me he would let me know what was going on when he found out more.

The next day, I called to check and see how everything was, and there was no change. Tuesday or Wednesday of that week, I was at practice. To get to our practice field, we had to go downstairs to the football field. Up above were the locker rooms and the administrative offices for the Athletic Department. It was at the beginning of practice, the middle of the week, and we were in stretching mode. I was facing the stairs that led down to our field, doing a straddle stretch in a seated position. I noticed the receptionist coming down the stairs, and it was strange considering she never left the office to come down onto the field.

She started at the top of the stairs and made her way down them. I was still stretching, but I couldn't take my eyes off her. When she made it down to the main practice level, she started walking across to the coaches. I looked at her and knew she was talking to them about me. I kept stretching and kept staring at her. I couldn't hear what she was saying because she was about seventy-five yards from me. I didn't know what they were saying, but I saw the coaches look around and then directly at me.

Coach Dennis Webb started walking toward me, and I just kept stretching and turned my eyes away from him. "Hey, V," he said, "come with me."

We both went upstairs toward the offices. One of the things embedded in all of the players was to never walk in the building with your cleats on. They warned us that if we did, we'd slip and fall and bust our butts and damage the floor in the meantime. It was something we just did not do, but this time, when I stopped at the bench to take my cleats off, the coach told me not to worry about it. At that point, I knew something was really wrong, and I got very concerned. For some reason, it did not dawn on me that it had to do with my father.

When I got into Coach Dennis Webb's office, he told me I needed to call home. My brother, Jemal, answered and broke the news to me. "Dad died today," he said. Jemal was also the one who had told me Mom died, and I can't imagine how he must have felt having to deliver such grim news a second time. I was standing up when I made the call, and once I got the news, I just sat down. Jemal explained that Dad couldn't recover from the stroke and it proved to be fatal. He asked me when I was coming back home, and I told him I'd be there as soon as I could.

Coach Webb's eyes were watery. He was a very compassionate man. I, on the other hand, didn't show any emotion. I was just very quiet. I had to stay strong because the first thing that came to my mind was what was going to happen to my family and to my brothers and sisters. That's all I cared about. I wasn't thinking about letting it out because at that time, we formed a pretty good bond, my father and I, and we were at a good place with one another. I genuinely loved the man, and losing him made me feel numb all over again. I just couldn't understand why all of these terrible things were happening to my family.

Before I left his office, Coach Webb told me the secretary was booking a flight for me right away. "We want you to come back, V," he said. "You have to come back." He looked at me with watery eyes and said, "For your family, you've got to come back. You hear me?"

I said, "Okay, Coach. I don't know what's going to happen with my family, but I'm going to try to come back."

I went to the dorm and started packing, and my teammate, Alvin Thomas, came in. He had heard about what happened. He was injured, so he wasn't at practice. He came in and just sat there and started crying. He just kept saying how sorry he was because he knew about my mom, and now my dad was gone too. His reaction touched me, and I finally broke down. He grabbed me and wouldn't let go. I think that was the only time I ever really broke down.

I got all packed and ready to go. Coach Webb drove me over to the airport. During that ride, I don't think we said two words for the whole thirty-five minutes. It's not that Coach Webb didn't want to talk, but he was just feeding off of me. I was pretty much stone-faced, and I didn't have anything to say. The only thing I kept thinking about was how I was going to keep my family together, so there was nothing much to say, and not a word was spoken.

At the airport, the coach walked with me right to the departing gate, because that was back when there were no airport security issues. He gave me a hug and said again, "V, you need to come back. You do whatever you have to do to come back. For so many reasons, you need to come back. I want to see you again."

"All I'm thinking about right now is my family," I told him. "I'm about to lose my family." Tears were rolling out of my eyes, and I noticed Coach Webb's eyes were pretty watery. I can't describe the type of pain I was feeling at that moment. My heart was literally torn in pieces. On the plane, all during the flight, I kept asking God, "Why? Why are you doing these terrible things to my family?" I started begging and pleading for Him to help me watch over my family.

Coach Olivieri picked me up at the airport. I really didn't have much to say to him either. I was silent and practically emotionless, a man on a mission. When we finally made it to my house, I greeted my brothers and sisters. Still, I remained stone-faced, focusing only on keeping my family together.

VERNON TURNER by Roland H. William

I had a lot on my mind during my college years.

Chapter 18:
"Make Sure You All Stay Together"

My father's side of the family made all the funeral arrangements. It was a difficult time for all of us, and my brothers and sisters were in a bad way. My sister, Sharlene, took it the hardest because she was old enough to understand what was going on. My brother, Jemal, was the closest to Dad, so it hit him pretty hard too. I really didn't have the time to break down again because I just needed to make sure my family was okay.

A couple days later, we had the funeral, and afterwards, all the family came back to the house. I noticed my Aunt Pat was there. She lived in Brooklyn on her own with her daughter. I pulled her aside and asked her if she would be able to stay at the house and take care of my family while I was away at school. She said, "Baby, I'll think about it. I don't know. Let me give it some thought."

I think it took me almost two weeks to get back to school. I know I missed the first week, but I did not want to leave until I knew my family was taken care of and that we were okay and weren't going to be split up.

My Aunt Pat stayed there while I was home. I was sitting on the porch with my head down, just thinking, when she came outside and told me, "Vernon, I'm going to stay here with the kids. Me and Carla, we'll move here and live at the house. You go on back to school." She also said, "I want you to get back to school now. I don't want you waiting anymore. You don't need to be here. There's nothing for you here. You get back to school now."

It sounded to me like Coach Webb might have called and spoken to Aunt Pat, but I could never be sure. I think he had a big influence on getting me back to school and having her stay. I also spoke to Coach Olivieri. He reassured me that everything was going to be fine and that I needed to get back to school. He said he'd do whatever he could to help me get back to Carson-Newman.

During the whole time I was at home, the people around me got an incorrect perception of how I was dealing with the death of my dad. I think they assumed that because of the issues I had years ago with my dad, I didn't care about him, especially because I didn't show any emotions during the funeral, before the funeral, at the wake, or after the funeral. I was just all business. All I was focusing on was trying to make sure my family was okay and that they stayed together, like my mother wanted. I didn't have time to grieve or mourn.

My sister, Sharlene, even asked me why I didn't cry. "You don't care?" she asked.

"I care," I told her. "I just don't have anything left. You know, I just want to make sure we're all together." It really hurt my feelings to know that I gave my brothers and sisters the wrong impression. They actually thought I didn't care, but it was really the total opposite. I made a promise to my mom that I'd keep the family together, and now there was no one else to see to that but me. My dad was gone, she was gone, and it was all on me. I was scared as hell about our situation.

Everything worked out though. I was able to go back to school and continue my education and my athletic career. When I went back to school, I was embraced. Everyone—coaches, players, and people in the town—were very compassionate about what happened. Everyone knew, even the people at the grocery stores. They were all so thoughtful of my feelings and everything that was going on with me and my family, and for the first time, the Southern hospitality really touched me and warmed my heart.

I knew I had to get back to business mentally. I had to flip the switch and get back to work on the football field and in the classroom. When I left to go to my dad's funeral and deal with my family issues, I was the starting tailback. I was gone for a week and a half and was able to make it to the following game. I only missed one game. Then, the following week, I got there by mid-week, on Wednesday. It was a testimony to the loyalty and dedication the program showed me, and it was also due to my hard work that they put me right back in the starting lineup. There wasn't even an issue by teammates or coaches. They just felt it was the right thing to do. I was touched by that because I didn't expect to come back and pick up where I had left off, but they insisted. Everything had to get back to where it was, and everyone wanted to make sure everything was back to normal for me, both mentally and physically.

There was a fantastic feeling of family within the program. I believe Coach Dennis Webb headed that effort, and I don't think he had an issue with Coach Ken Sparks. He was pretty adamant about what should be done. The way Coach Ken Sparks is, I'm sure he jumped right on board and there was not even an issue. I'm eternally grateful for them making that move. There was no telling what would've happened if they would have handled me with kid gloves and treated me different, but they didn't do that. It was business as usual, and VT was back. That made the transition back to school and football much smoother, and even though in many ways my world changed again when my dad died, it stayed the same at Carson-Newman because of a few great and caring men.

Chapter 19:
Working Through the Tough Times

The one person that helped me throughout my whole college career that I've not yet mentioned was Lynda Hill. All the athletes called her 'Mom.' You will not find a more decent and fine woman than Lynda. She was an administrative assistant for Academic Affairs. She loved sports and attended all the sporting events. She had two young boys named Skip and Reaux, and they were with her wherever she went. They were two little hellions on the surface, as some boys tend to be, but they were good kids underneath. They flocked to the ball players, and all the athletes knew the kids. Their mother was something special. She cooked for us and helped us study, and anytime we needed her for anything, she was there. She was our mom away from home in every way, a woman so full of unconditional love.

I will never, ever forget all the things Lynda did to help me during my college years. She was simply unbelievable. To this day, we keep in touch: an email here or a phone call there. She's still doing the same thing, still involved, still doing her thing and helping out those young athletes. All I can say about Mom Hill is that she was a godsend and a lifesaver for me.

I had a solid season my freshman year under the circumstances. I finished with just under 600 yards and a few touchdowns. During the off-season, I tried to live in the weight room, but that particular off-season was pretty tough because I had to be the disciplinary person over the telephone with my brothers and sisters. I would constantly get phone calls from my aunt informing me that Jemal was doing this or Brian was doing that, Ellen was a pain in the ass, and Sharlene wouldn't listen because she thought she was grown. I got those phone calls almost on a daily basis.

So, my focus was still heavily on my family and trying to make sure nothing got out of hand because my biggest scare was that my aunt would get fed up and just leave. For that reason, I was always on my brothers' and sisters' cases via telephone. I would really be on them during the off-season and holidays when I went home.

I got on them and stayed on them. I was really scared my aunt would say she'd had enough and leave, and I needed her to stay.

My sophomore season was pretty difficult for several reasons. First off, I was barely getting by with my grades. Second, Ken Tyson came back off injury and took the starting spot back, so I wasn't starting anymore. To be perfectly honest, I really couldn't complain. Ken was the best running back in the nation; he had to start. He was tremendous and quite deserving of the starting spot. At that time, he was a better tailback than I was.

While I was dealing with that demotion of sorts, I was also still trying to keep my family intact and in line from a distance. I continuously had to make sure they were doing the right things back in Staten Island. During my sophomore year, I played perhaps four to five games the entire season, and even those weren't full games because I was just a backup for Kenny Tyson. He ended up getting hurt again at the end of the season. We went to the National Championship, but we lost. I did play quite a bit that game, but by that time I just wasn't really mentally into it. It was just a busted season for me, and at the end of the Championship Game, I went home and had a talk with my high school football coach, Fred Olivieri. I told him I couldn't focus and that it had been a really tough season for me. I didn't know if I even wanted to go back. I was just really out of it.

But within a few minutes, Fred refocused me, as he had a gift for doing. He said, "What are you going to do here, V? What are you going to do here if you don't go back to school? Are you going to support your family by flipping burgers? I mean, what are you going to do? You have to go back and rededicate yourself. Just think about all the hard work that you've done to this point. Think about all the things you've gone through. Think about all the extra training. You woke up in the middle of the night and did workouts just so you could stay a step ahead of your opponents. There is no harder worker than you. I've never met a young man or any individual that works as hard as you. It is understandable why you lost your focus. It's totally understandable, but what is not acceptable is you quitting. I did not train a quitter. I did not teach you to quit, Vernon Turner, and I'll be damned if you quit now." Then he went on to say, "What are you going to do? You are going to take this little time you have at home, spend it with the family, and rededicate yourself. Set yourself some new goals and do whatever you have to do to attain those goals!"

Coach O reenergized me. I was like a dead battery, and he recharged me. After that pep talk from him, I could not wait to get to school in Tennessee, but before I left, I took a walk in the park. I had to rededicate myself after all the regrets for all the things I had done. I had to rededicate the last two years of my college career, and when I got home from that very same park where I had first learned to love the game of football, I had my new dedication. "I'll do it for Mom and Dad," I told myself. The man I had lost was no longer my stepfather; he was my dad, and I missed Mom and him dearly. I wanted to dedicate the rest of my college career to them, and that's just what I did.

That's all there was to it. All the regrets, all the things I had done—like wishing my mom dead and not getting along with my father because he was White and argued with my mom all the time, and arguing with both of them before they died—those are things I'm going to take to my grave. Before their last breaths, I didn't offer them an "I love you" or even a proper goodbye, and I fought with both of them right before they died. I'll have to live with that for the rest of my life, but at that moment, I rededicated myself.

When I got back to school, I was a different person. My training regimen was vigorous. I beefed up to 175 pounds. I was very driven and extremely determined. I went back to my old training regimens from in high school. I set my alarm clock for early in the morning, before classes, in order to get a weight room workout or do two sets of fifty push-ups. I went back to being one step ahead of my opponent. I went back to the old V and those Jedi mind tricks. I thought, *If I look good and feel good, there is a great chance I will play well.*

I was determined to do well on behalf of the dedication I had made to my parents. God must have heard me talking to Him, because I got less calls from my aunt complaining about my brothers and sisters. They seemed to have themselves together, and that allowed me to be able to focus more on my studies and football. That whole year, I was totally focused. On the night before opening day, I stenciled 'Mom' and 'Dad' on a towel I wore, along with my nickname, 'Chill' and the number '1,230.' I don't even know where the number came from, but I knew that was how many yards I was going to run that year. With that towel by my side and my focus and dedication intact game after game after game, I was putting up numbers, scoring touchdowns, breaking long runs, and running with a vengeance. It was one of the best years of my whole football career!

Chapter 20:
National Championship

We qualified to go to the National Championship all four years of my college career, and we won it every year with the exception of my sophomore year. During my junior year, we were lighting it up. I was having a fantastic year, running like a madman. In the second round of the playoffs, I forgot who we were playing, but I remember taking a pitch (a sweep play). We were on our own thirty-yard line. I took the pitch from Easy-E, I turned that corner, and I was gone! I took it seventy yards to pay dirt. I remember hearing over the loudspeaker, "Vernon Turner has just eclipsed over 1,000 yards rushing!" That was tremendous for me because I knew I had two more games to reach my mark.

We were in playoff mode, so if we lost any game, we were out. It was one and done, simple as that. We made it past the first round, and the next game was against Central State of Ohio. That was a tough game. They were probably one of the best teams we played. I think I gained just over fifty yards, but we did pull out a victory and advanced to the National Championship game.

The one thing I was thinking about was that I needed to run as hard as I could every time I touched the football. That week of practice, I was so focused and tensed that the blocking schemes had to be perfect for me. Again, we only ran about ten to twelve plays, but we ran those plays to perfection. But I took it further; I wanted it to be automatic. From the time I got out of my stance, I wanted to go full speed at my line and know they were going to make the block. I often stayed after practice with the linemen to make sure they knew how fast I was going to go. Edwin, the quarterback, was out there as well. It was something I had never done before, but I was so focused. I was so keen and in tune to making sure we were on point. None of the coaches said anything about it, so I can only assume they were impressed. They never interfered and were always encouraging us. They were just as focused because they wanted the best. They wanted us to be perfect that day.

I broke into open field my junior year at Carson-Newman.

My junior year in college. Head Coach, Ken Sparks,
and I show love before the play-off game.

When the big Saturday arrived, my family surprised me. My brother, his best friend, the assistant coach, Bob McGhie, and someone else (that I unfortunately cannot remember all these years later) showed up to watch that game. It was a cold day because it had snowed the day before, but they still drove twelve to thirteen hours in the nasty winter weather to come and see me play in that Championship Game. I found out the night before that they were there. I was so happy to see my people finally getting a chance to see me play college football. You would think it would've added pressure on me, but I was so focused and determined already that I was just happy they were there to see it all go down.

I had a ritual before each game: I would go outside, with my Walkman on, and walk a lap around the football field, staying inside, and made sure I touched every corner of the end zone, and then I would walk back in the locker room. I guess it caught on, because my quarterback, Edwin Lowery, who I became real close friends with during my college years, started doing it with me. We never talked; we just walked the field. At the end of the walk, Edwin always said, "This is your game, baby. This is your game. This is you, V. You worked too hard… too hard this week. This is all you, baby. You're going to make something happen." I just nodded at him and went back into the locker room and started getting dressed. I did mention he was a hyper one, right?

In the locker room, I didn't speak to anyone. I don't recall having one single conversation during the course of suiting up. I was completely and utterly focused, thinking about running hard every time I touched the football. I was thinking six points, thinking about the blocking scheme we had been going over so relentlessly for the whole past week. I was thinking about how my guard and tackle were coming down the block, and I was going to come right off my tackle's butt, right off his ass, at full speed. That's all I thought about because that's all we did. We had three- to four-foot splits between our guards and tackles. We forced the defense to spread their defensive line, which gave me a running lane. Our linemen were so fast! They would crash down so fast on the down block, and with my speed, it created a natural lane. If I hit it fast enough and hard enough, no one could touch us. That was all I thought about in that locker room that day. I just sat there thinking about that down block and running off my tackle's ass, getting full speed by the time I hit the line of scrimmage. That's all we had worked so hard on all week, and that's all I thought about.

We won the coin toss, and they kicked the ball off. They kicked it in the back of the end zone, and we started the offensive series on our own twenty-yard line. I remember Easy-E calling the play, Black 22, a dive option right. I was the tailback on the left-hand side, and I was going to be the option back, going to the right side. We stepped up to the line, and it was so embedded in us that we knew he was going to call an audible because of the alignment of the defensive lineman. Robert Thomas, the other tailback, and I walked up to the line of scrimmage and looked at one another. We knew he was about to call the audible, White 22 or Orange 22, a dive option left. So, I became the dive back, and I knew by the alignment of that defense that he was going to hand the ball off and I was going to get it. I also knew by the alignment of that defense how my guard and my tackle were going to down block and how I was going to come off that down block. I already had it in my head, just how fast I was going to run off my tackle's ass. We had practiced it that whole year; especially that week... and it came out beautifully!

Edwin came out to the line. "Easy, easy, easy... White 22, White 22!" — A dive option left, just like we thought. On his second "Hut!" I came out like a rocket. My guard and tackle blocked down. They crashed down on the defensive tackle and the nose guard. The defensive end was sitting there, and Edwin had to read that defensive end, but that defensive end was sitting so far out wide that Edwin had to give it to me, and I knew that. Edwin gave me that ball, and the next thing I knew, I was at the fifty-yard line. I ended up going into the end zone, eighty yards untouched, and that was just the first play of the game. That set the tempo and the tone for the kind of game I was going to have.

I ended up with seventeen carries, three touchdowns, and 189 yards that game. It was a very emotional game for me, especially the second half. My teammates knew how important the game was for me because I'd been practically silent all week and was completely focused. During the course of the game, the guys noticed tears in my eyes because I was just trying so hard to accomplish the goals I had set in honor of my parents. Evidentially, they kept track of what I did, because they did not let me leave that game until I achieved that goal.

Every time I made a run with the ball, the linemen picked me up and gave me a hug. They saw how emotional I was during the course of the game, and that made them work even harder in helping me achieve my goal. That was really special to me. Once I got the yards I needed, they gave me a standing ovation. After I walked off the field, I really broke down. I went to the bench and put a towel over my head and just bawled like a baby. The embrace I received from my teammates, coaches, and everyone else that day was something I will never forget. To put it lightly, it was an unbelievable game for me and my team, and everyone took notice.

I was fortunate enough to be honored with the award for the Offensive Player MVP of the Championship Game, another special memory. I ended up driving back with my family that night, and it was a really good feeling to be able to take that achievement home and share it with my relatives and friends back in Staten Island. My junior year in college was a really special year. I rededicated myself mentally and physically, and I turned it around. A great deal of that had to do with Fred Olivieri refocusing me. If it wasn't for him, I don't know if I would've been able to refocus myself. I could say thanks to Fred a thousand times, and it still would not be enough gratitude for what he did for me by not letting me quit.

Chapter 21:
Getting Personal

A social life in Jefferson City, Tennessee, wasn't so easy to come by for a twenty-year-old Black guy from New York. There wasn't anything to do in that predominantly White area. We had to travel over thirty miles just to go to the mall; the hot spot in town was McDonalds, and even that was fairly new. As far as dating went, it was inevitable that the Black athletes had to date White girls because they were all that was available to us if we wanted to date at all. By then, I had gotten past my prejudices against Whites. In fact, my high school sweetheart was White, so the difference in race was no longer an issue for me. Still, at that time, interracial dating wasn't generally socially accepted, particularly in the South. That's just the way it was. I wasn't necessarily proud of myself for leaving home to pursue an academic and athletic career, but once I got there, I really went buck wild.

It was toward the end of my junior year when I started to break out of my shell—to the extreme. I guess you could say I was promiscuous, pretty much out of control. I slept with anyone I could. As a result of my lewd behavior, I ended up fathering a child during my junior year of college. It's rather embarrassing to admit this now, but looking back, I was completely out of control!

Being a 'baby daddy' was something I wasn't prepared or ready for in the least, but the baby's mother had no intention of having an abortion, so I had to step up and do what I had to do. I was young and stupid back then, but it was something that happened, and I had to deal with it. Becoming a father was a wake-up call for me, and it was pretty intense. On June 9, 1988, my daughter, Ashley, was born. She turned out to be a pretty damn good kid, albeit not with my help. Her mother ended up raising her pretty much on her own and did a fantastic job with her.

As I mentioned before, I was pretty wild when it came to my social life, especially during my junior and senior years. It was pretty crazy. Even though I was already a dad, I saw several young ladies, to be perfectly honest, but there was one in particular that I saw more than the others. By the end of my senior year, the girl I was seeing informed me that she was pregnant. This time, I was in denial. I could not believe it had happened again. I kept telling her, "The baby's not mine. It has to be somebody else's," but deep down, I knew better. I knew I was the father. She was a really good girl by comparison to some of her classmates, and I knew I was the only one she had been with. But still, I refused to believe it. Because I convinced myself it was not my child, I turned my back on the mother and simply ignored the fact that I was going to be a father for the second time. That was probably one of the worst things I've ever done in my life—turning my back on a child that I knew was mine. To this day, I regret it.

Nineteen years later, a young man found me on Facebook. His name is Darris. I didn't think anything of it because young athletes from all over the place often contact me asking for training tips or wanting me to train them for their upcoming seasons, but there was something different about Darris. The questions he asked got me thinking. In between what seemed like normal sports questions, he would throw in random questions about my family and how many kids I have.

Considering how paranoid I've always been about people getting in my personal business, there was something about Darris that just made me want to be 100 percent honest with him. I answered all of his questions and told him I have two kids, a girl and a boy. I told him I never met my son and that I turned my back on him and his mom nineteen years earlier. I explained to Darris that the more time that went by, the harder it was to reach out to them. I told him I would never forgive myself for turning my back on my son and that I would never even deserve to have any type of relationship with him. I told him that with each passing year, it ate at my heart, knowing I had a son out there who didn't even know me. I was convinced I was going to hell for this, and I told Darris that.

I had never talked to anyone about it, not until this young man messaged me through Facebook. Darris waited for about three days to respond, and at this point, I didn't know who he was. Sometime during the evening, I received an email from Darris, and he said, "What if I told you that you are corresponding with your son right now? My name is Joshua Darris."

I had known all along that my son's name was Joshua, but Darris went by his middle name, and that really threw me. I was speechless to find this out, and before I got a chance to respond, he emailed back and said, "I forgive you. I forgave you a long time ago. I just want to get to know you now." I don't have the words to explain how I felt at that particular time. I was completely overcome with relief, gratefulness, and disbelief all at once.

Since then, my son, Darris, and I have been communicating, and I have to say his mother has done an unbelievable job raising him. He's a terrific young man, as is evidenced by the fact that he wanted someone like me in his life even after I'd put him through a lifetime of being ignored and neglected by his father. That alone says a lot about this young man's character and about the amazing mother who raised him.

In spite of all the partying and going out, one thing I never did was take drugs—not even dope. I did drink some alcohol, but that was the craziest thing I ever did. I had seen what that shit did to my mother, and I wasn't about to succumb to that kind of lifestyle. My vice was girls, plain and simple, and looking back now, I know I should have been more responsible to myself and the lives that I touched and created. Fortunately, we live and learn.

My daughter, Ashley.

My son, Darris.

*I was honored with the Sportsman of the Year
award on Staten Island.*

Chapter 22:
A New Game Plan—Going Pro

Things changed, as they tend to do when we are young adults. Just before the Championship Game (my senior year), during the playoffs, I received a phone call from my Aunt Pat, who was staying at my house while I was in school. She told me she was financially and mentally drained and that she simply could not manage to take care of my siblings anymore. "We're not going to make it, baby," she said. "We're going to have to split the kids apart and live in different places."

My heart dropped to my stomach when I got this distressing news, as if my worst nightmare had just come true. I begged and pleaded with her not to leave until I could figure out some things. "Is it a money thing?" I asked her. "Let me make some phone calls, Auntie, and do whatever I have to do. At least let me finish school before you do anything. Please!" I begged. I didn't want my family split apart because we were so close. I think I literally hung up on her by accident just so I could start making phone calls.

The first person I called—the only person, actually—was my high school football coach. I filled him in on what was going on. All he said was, "You just focus on your school, V. I will do what I can to help out over here. Just worry about finishing up school. I got your back. I'll make sure everything is okay."

I called my aunt back and told her to take down Coach Olivieri's number and call him if she needed anything at all. I promised her I would try and gather up some money on my end and send it to her. "Whenever you need money… whenever you need anything, we'll make sure you get it," I promised. "Just hang in there, Auntie, and let me finish school." I told her she could leave if she wanted, but I didn't want my family broken apart.

After hearing how desperate I was to finish what I started at Carson-Newman, she selflessly agreed to stay. I was blessed with an amazing family.

Right then and there, my focus changed. I got scared—really scared. I could not, in good conscience, rely on my high school football coach to support my family; he had his own family, and I just couldn't let him do that. I was really concerned and scared and didn't know what to do, so I started cutting hair and giving therapeutic massages on the side. Whatever money I made went right to my aunt back in New York. Just before the semi-finals round of the playoffs, my mind was a little jacked up, but I had learned a long time before that how to flip the switch. I learned how to put aside those outside distractions and keep focused on football. I ended up having a good semi-final game and a good National Championship Game.

It wasn't anything like my junior year, but under the circumstances, I still gave a solid performance. My college career was over after that, but honestly, as soon as that fourth quarter ticked down and the game was over, I was already putting together a game plan for what I was going to do next. The day after the Championship Game, I decided that I had to try out to play professional football. I decided right then and there that it was something I HAD to do. It wasn't just that I wanted to because it was a childhood dream of mine. I felt like I had no other option if I wanted to keep my family together like I had promised Mom. I had to make it in pro ball, and while it was deadly frightening to me, that's all I thought about from that moment on.

Chapter 23:
Preparing for the NFL (1989)

That following weekend, after the Championship Game, I went directly to Coach Fred's house, and I informed him I was going to try out for the NFL. He just looked at me and without any hesitation said, "Okay. If that's the case, we need to get you an agent. Let me call Dino."

Dino Mangeiro had enjoyed a really long career as a defensive lineman for the Kansas City Chiefs. He was also an alum of my high school, Curtis High, so that was our 'in' to finding a good agent. Coach called Dino, and Dino gave us the number to his agent.

The agent's name was Tony Agnone, and his partner was Howard Shatsky; the two of them were known around the league for specializing in small college football players—both those that came from small colleges and those that were small in stature. At the time, some of his bigger-name clients were Dave Meggett, a running back and return specialist for the New York Giants. They also had Sean Landeta, the Giants punter. We had a half-hour phone conference with Tony, and by the time we got done with that conversation, everyone was onboard. As far as all of us were concerned, it was a good fit, and we needed to do it.

They informed me that I needed to start training and get ready to play different positions that I wasn't used to playing. They told me I needed to hone up on my wide receiver skills and especially my punt catching skills. They already had a game plan in mind. Basically, that's what Dave Meggett had to do; he worked on catching punts, but he stayed at the running back position. Tony and Howard didn't think I would make it as a running back in the NFL because of my size, so I had to focus on honing my skills as a wide receiver and punt returner.

My new agents were also informed of my work ethic, and they named me 'the Warrior.' All throughout my tenure with them, I kept that nickname, which was quite fitting because it fell right in line with my high school mascot. That was the very start of my pro career, but it was a difficult journey to say the least.

When I made the decision to turn pro, it was something I simply had to do. I now had a really good agent, but that was the easy part. The hard part was going to be getting noticed. Because I attended a small college, I didn't get the same type of media coverage that I would have had I gone to a major university, so getting my name out there and showing what I was capable of was our next step in our game plan.

Chapter 24:
A Letter from Sweetness and a Payton-Worthy Regimen

I took a total of two and a half weeks off after the Championship Game, and then I was right back to work. I had my own personal training camp, which lasted for eight weeks, three training sessions a day. I wouldn't recommend my training regimen to anyone, not even my worst enemies. It was probably one of the mentally and physically toughest training regimens I ever endured, mainly because of where I got the idea from.

I've mentioned Walter Payton several times through the writing of this book because he was my ultimate role model, my childhood idol, and someone I really looked up to. It was the way he carried himself on and off the field that made Walter an inspiration in every sense of the world. Whatever he did and whatever he said was gospel to me. Preach it, Payton!

Now facing my attempt to break into Walter's turf, the NFL, I said to myself, "V, what have you got to lose?" While looking through a football magazine in the college library, I saw one of Walter's fan club listings; it guaranteed he would read his fan mail. I wrote to him at the address listed in the magazine. I started off by telling him how much he had inspired me. I told him how I tried to mimic his style of playing football and that I appreciated him as a person. I also told him about my situation, my family background, and what my family and I were going though. Since he went to Jackson State, a small school like mine, I also told him I had gone to Carson-Newman. I wanted Walter Payton to know what I was trying to do, and I asked him if he had any words of encouragement or any advice he could give that would help me adjust and compete at the next level. I made sure he knew I'd appreciate any words from him.

About three weeks later, I was astounded to receive a letter back from Walter Payton. Just as he spoke in public, he spoke to me on paper. My jaw literally dropped. I couldn't believe my eyes. I just sat there for about two minutes, staring at the letter. I said to myself, "I'm communicating with my idol. Oh my God! This is a letter from Sweetness... from THE Walter Payton—right here in my hand!"

Walter thanked me for the kind words and for writing him. He also thanked me for sharing my most personal experiences regarding my family, and he offered his condolences to me for the loss of my mom and dad. In his letter, he emphasized never giving up. He wrote a few words that I will never forget: "The mental toughness has to be just as solid as your physical toughness. In fact, you have to have more mental toughness than you have physical toughness. The biggest part of your body is your heart. Someone who has a big heart is going to achieve more than someone that doesn't."

He went on to give me some of his training regimens. "Because of your size, you'll need to focus on developing your explosiveness, quickness, and speed. The first thing you need to do is start running a lot of hills." He told me to get a good pair of heavy boots and run hills in them. He also told me to run a lot in sand. He said it would help me develop my explosiveness and power. He went on to say that running in the water would develop muscles in my body that I rarely used. In addition, I was advised to attach a long piece of rope to a tire and run straight sprints to help improve my power and explosiveness. He wanted me to do all my training with resistance.

One workout in particular that he suggested makes me laugh now, but it wasn't funny back then. He told me to find a wooded field with a lot of trees—"good, strong trees." I must admit, when I first read that I needed to make sure they were "good, strong trees," the first thing that came to mind was that I would have to climb them. He told me to make sure the wooded field was between 80 and 100 yards in radius, preferably a flat surface. He said, "You need to go on one end of that field, with football in hand, and run through it to the other side as fast as you can through the trees." I needed to elude the trees without breaking stride, while running full speed. If I fell or hit a tree, I was to get up and continue running. Again, I can laugh about it now, but I wasn't laughing then. I could only do it once a week because that's how long it took for the knots to go down that found their way to the top of my head from hitting trees. I was dinged up pretty bad. My shins, my forehead, and my arms were bruised. My body looked like it had been dragged down the street for a half mile. I did that once a week for approximately six weeks, and it was no joke, no matter how funny it must have looked.

The additional training regimens Sweetness gave me, coupled with the things I was already doing (weight lifting, agility drills, punt and pass catching drills), made me untouchable by the time I got on a football field. When I was going against the other players in training camp, one pro coach described me as being "quick as a hiccup." That's pretty quick, and it was one heck of a compliment. Still, I didn't have the same opportunity all the big school athletes had or even the players that were projected to go pro from my school. They had scouts coming to the school and asking them to work out, and they were being pulled out of classes. Some of them even got invited to the combine and senior bowl games. I had my work cut out for me if I was going to stand out in the crowd.

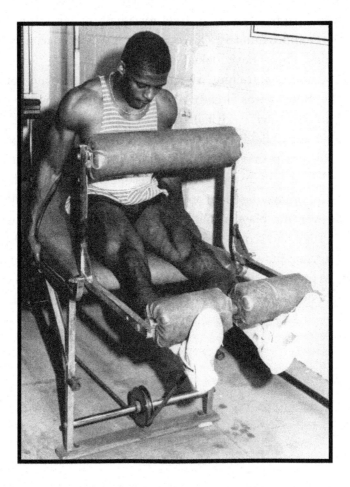

I put my body through hell preparing for the NFL.

Chapter 25:
Workouts for the Pro Scouts and Draft Day Blues

I didn't have the unbelievable stats in college, and I didn't get invited to a combine. I didn't go to any All-Star games. No one was asking for me at the start, and no one was asking to see me run, but Tony and Howard already knew what was going to happen for me. Hell, it wasn't there first rodeo.

They already knew all of the stuff I was about to go through. They said, "V, you're going to have to go the long way to make it. You're going to have to go through hell." They went on to say, "But you're going to already have half the battle won because you're going to be mentally prepared for what's about to happen because we're going to tell you. You're probably going to end up working out between thirty-eight to fifty times for various teams."

The reason I had to work out that many times is because I wasn't going to be invited to the combine. At the combine, all I would have had to do was work out a couple of times, and then I'd be done. The combine was where every scout for every team was going to be. I wasn't invited to any of the senior bowl games where they could have seen me compete against the other top athletes across the country. My agents told me I would not have that luxury. "They're just going to be able to see your film and see what you do in the workouts you're going to have to do." So, I was going to have to be on point during those thirty-eight to fifty workouts.

I was also informed that the pro scouts were not going to ask for me in the beginning. "What's going to happen is," my agents told me, "you're going to have your carry-on bag with your workout clothes, and when you see your teammates get pulled out of class or if you hear through the grapevine that some scouts are there, just go on out there with the rest of the players."

They told me something that surprised me: "One thing a scout will never do is that he will never turn down an athlete who wants to work out, because they believe in finding a diamond in the rough. So, when you go to them and say you want to run for them, they are going to say yes. No one is ever going to say no." And, my agents were right.

Anytime I saw my teammates go out there to work out, I was right there. I had my bag with me and asked the scouts if they minded if I ran. The first team I ran for was the Buffalo Bills. I went up to the Bills scout and asked him, "Do you mind if I run?"

He said, "No, go ahead. Go with the rest of them."

Of course, I went last. The top prospect at our school was defensive back David Pool, who ran in the low 4.3's in his forty-yard dash. Brent Collins, a linebacker, ran just under 4.8, and our other defensive backs, Joe Fishback and Sammy Dixon, both ran between 4.5 and 4.65. Those were all really good times for their perspective positions.

Then, there was me. Everything I'd been doing during the course of my time there was about to be exposed. I'd been in my training camp mode for the last four and a half weeks, and I'd been doing three workouts a day, everything in resistance, running through trees, running up hills, and running with a tire around my waist, obeying every word Walter told me. This time, though, I wasn't wearing heavy steel-toed boots. I wasn't running uphill or dragging tires all over the place. There was no extra weight on my body to tug around. It was just me and my running shoes. So, when I took off, from that starting line, I felt ten times faster than I had the last time I ran. When I crossed the finish line and looked back, I saw the scouts do a double-take on the watch. I knew then that I had them—I just knew it! When they asked me to run again, I did, and again they did a double-take. In the forty-yard dash, I ran a 4.39 and a 4.37. Before I started my Sweetness-inspired hellish training regimen, I was running in the mid 4.5s.

In addition to the forty-yard dash, the scouts took us through a bench press test, the vertical jump, and a shuttle run—not to mention catching passes and punts. I had to document all of that on a chart I made. I wrote down the results of my forty-yard times and my agility results. Then, I had to call my agents with those results, and they kept their own records. They used those results to call various teams to inform them of what I was doing. When the scouts showed up after that, they started asking for little ol' me, believe it or not. My agents and I were feeling pretty good about the way things were going. The game plan was working, and we were really excited about the results of my training regimens. It was really working out. We felt pretty confident that I had gone from a no-name to a potential mid-round draft pick; even Mel Kiper (an NFL draft analyst), called me 'a sleeper' and said I should be a mid-round pick. My speed, agility drills, and everything I had done paid off, and I was a sleeper. I was pretty excited about it, but that was an unfortunate deal because now I had it in my head that I would be getting drafted and I had my hopes up.

I took two and a half weeks off after the title game in college...
then I started getting ready for the NFL.

On Draft Day, I was on the college campus at Mom Lynda Hill's house. I had given my agents her number. We had a little Draft Day get-together with some friends. I would have bet everything I had that I was going to be drafted. I worked out a total of forty-three times for almost every team in the National Football League, and I had a bunch of fantastic workouts. My body was exhausted, but I couldn't worry about that; I had way too much at stake.

The first day of the draft came and went with no calls, but I didn't anticipate a call on the first day anyway. Then, the second day came and went and went: seventh round, eighth round, and ninth round. The more rounds that went by, the more depressed I got and the more disappointed I was. The next thing I knew, the draft was over, and my name was never called. I was kind of embarrassed because I had tooted my horn a little bit, telling people I was most likely going to be drafted in the mid-rounds. To be honest, I kind of set myself up for a letdown, and it was a letdown indeed.

Shortly after the draft, my agent called and informed me there were about five teams interested in signing me. Being the great and thoughtful and experienced agents that they were, they wanted to find the best fit, the best place where I could most likely make the team. They thought that team was the Denver Broncos.

Ricky Nattiel, Vance Johnson, and Mark Jackson, the main receivers on the Denver Broncos at that time, were called 'Three Amigos' by the media. Ricky Nattiel had a season-ending knee injury the year before, and they weren't sure if he was going to make it or not. Ricky wasn't looking good at all in the off-season, and it didn't look too promising for him. My agents thought Ricky's unfortunate injury might work to my benefit. The Denver Broncos also didn't have a kickoff or punt return guy, so that would've worked out really well.

I told my agents, "Okay, let's do this." I flew to Denver, to their mini-camp, and signed with the Denver Broncos. That day in Colorado, my pro career started.

I put my body through absolute hell!

Fourth Quarter

*Me and Shannon Sharpe at the Denver Broncos'
training camp our rookie year.*

Chapter 26:
Broncos Training Camp

After I received the phone call from my agents informing me that there were a few teams interested in signing me as a free agent after the draft, I got word that the best candidate was the Denver Broncos. Because of their need, we made the decision to sign a contract with them. I still wasn't happy overall in regards to not getting drafted, but that ended once I received a phone call from Coach Fred Olivieri. He reminded me of the big picture of getting that opportunity and that I'd already managed to beat the odds. I'll never forget that conversation because he knew exactly what I was thinking and how I was feeling. I guess he realized that I actually needed a phone call from him just to make sure I was okay and that I needed some reassurance, but that conversation was just another door opening for me to see a light. Again, he informed me that I'd worked too hard to get to where I was, and playing for Denver was a rare opportunity of grand proportions. He reminded me of the countless times I had taken advantage of every opportunity and told me, "You aren't going to stop now." That was a turning point for me in heading to the next level. By the time I got done speaking with Fred on the phone, I was already rejuvenated and refocused.

I remember getting off the plane in Denver, the Mile-High City, and being greeted by one of the scouts. It was the first team workout after the draft, and they wanted to get all the players together as soon as possible. In fact, if I'm not mistaken, Coach Dan Reeves, our coach at the time, summoned everyone at the mini-camp. Arriving during the day and having our first team meeting that same evening was an experience in itself, especially since I didn't know anyone on the team. I wouldn't say I was star struck because I was pretty focused, but I started to remember watching The Three Amigos on TV, probably the most fearful trio of wide receivers in the league. They were some pretty awesome cats to watch, and what amazed me when I first saw them at camp was how small they were. I don't think any of them eclipsed over five-ten, but they were all productive in their own way.

Vance Johnson was extremely fast and smooth when it came to route running. I'd say Mark Jackson was hardnosed, tough, and fearless when going across the middle. He was always known for making the tough catches; he was something to watch. Ricky Nattiel was just an overall deceptive athlete, which works well in football. The defensive backs underestimated him all the time, and the next thing they knew, he'd be open and catching big balls. And then, there was the QB launching balls to these guys. What more can you say about Elway? The first time I met John Elway in person, I noticed two things: he was a pretty big guy, and he had some long teeth on him. I just kept staring at his mouth and thought to myself, *Goodness gracious! Elway has teeth the size of a full-grown horse!* Of course, I'd never say that to the man's face because he deserved utmost respect for the way he played the game.

My amateurish awe changed the following day when we got on the field. During our first team meeting, we were addressed by future Hall of Famer, Dan Reeves. From day one, everyone knew that man meant business. I knew right out of the gate that we all had to take care of our business, and I had the advantage since I was often underestimated. Believe it or not, people would look at it from the outside and say, "Oh, Turner, you don't have a chance in hell," but one of the other things my high school coach and my agents, Tony and Howard, had mentioned to me was that I was what you might call 'a major underdog.' The thing most people failed to realize was that I had been an underdog all my life and I had worked my ass off for everything I had. I had been fighting with my back up against the wall since I was eight years old, and to be perfectly honest, I wouldn't have it any other way.

One thing you have to realize is that professional athletics is a business, whether it's football, baseball, basketball, hockey, or anything else, it's all about making and saving money and winning games. My agents reminded me that if I could be that diamond in the rough and be productive against the big-time college goers, the Pro Bowlers, and the guys that were making millions of dollars, I would have a great chance in earning a spot on the final roster.

I'm in my very first training camp in the NFL (Denver Broncos).

It didn't make sense to me, really, because I wasn't thinking in that aspect. I was certain they would keep those guys playing because they had invested a lot of money in them, but other than that, I wasn't thinking in business terms. If a team can get a guy at lower pay with just as much ability, they're more than likely going to get rid of a player that's making $1.5 million dollars and keep a player that's making $250,000 dollars with the same potential, if not better.

That's what I was constantly reminded of. The more they said it, the more it made sense, but my mind was on a different track. I wanted to compete, and I wanted to earn a spot regardless of who was making what. As far as I was concerned, second sucked, and I didn't want to be second to anyone—paychecks aside. I wanted to play based on my skills and not on the fact that I was a bargain for the team.

In that meeting, Dan Reeves set his expectations, and he made it clear that we had to earn a spot on his team. Every player had to show his net worth, and Reeves said he would only put the best players on the football field, regardless of who they were. It seemed to me like the kind of thing most coaches would have to say in order to get the best out of their athletes. It was politically correct, and even though you wouldn't think a coach would bench a John Elway, if he's not doing well, it would be the right thing to do. Everything Coach Reeves said held true. He reminded us that we were in the NFL, the National Football League, but it also stood for 'Not For Long,' and if we didn't handle our business on the field, we wouldn't be around long.

I can't recall all the rookies that came in my year, but I remember Blake Ezor out of Michigan State because he was a running back and wasn't as big as I thought. He was only about five-nine and 190 pounds with his equipment on, and I found that surprising. He was about the same size as me, and I found it a bit unsettling that I was forced to change my position due to my size while he wasn't. I figured he must've put up some good stats at a big-time school, and that gave him the advantage of not having to change his position.

Shannon Sharpe is one of the few names that stand out in my mind. He was a wide receiver out of Savannah State, and it was his rookie season as well. Shannon was a beast from day one. He came into the Broncos camp as a wide receiver, but in my opinion, he was too slow for it. Then again, he was too doggone fast to be a tight end. Sharpe was one of those in-between players, one of those kids coming out of college that was extremely strong on and off the football field. He practically lived in the weight room, and having a brother like Sterling Sharpe didn't exactly hurt him at all. It's safe to say he had a solid pedigree. Shannon took care of his business on the field, and between his blocking and catching ability, it was difficult to tackle him. Off the field, he had a personality that could win anyone over. He was always smiling and obviously had the gift of gab. He was just fun to be around. Shannon and I got along pretty well. I know for a fact that if I called him up today and said, "Hey, man, this is VT, remember me from our rookie year over at Denver?" he'd start just cracking up, because you never forget where it all started, and we went through all that crazy rookie-year stuff together.

They didn't do too much hazing back then because Coach Reeves didn't approve, but we had to do skits and recite things during the course of training camp. One of the things we had to do was perform in front of the veterans on the stage. It didn't matter what it was, but we had to do something. Shannon, a few other guys, and I got together and did a skit of *Harlem Nights*. If I'm not mistaken, we reenacted the first scene of the movie—a nightclub scene when Richard Pryor, Red Foxx, and a few of the other actors were around a table rolling dice. Our version of it had those guys rolling on the floor; it really was that hilarious, and of course Shannon Sharpe stole the show. I'm usually pretty shy when it comes to stuff like that, but it was a lot of fun making a fool of myself on that stage with those guys, and it's something I don't think any of us will ever forget. We rookies bonded pretty well because we always had to do things together, whether it was carrying the veteran's equipment or just singing random song on command. We went through some really wild stuff together.

The first day of mini-camp was an eye opener in regards to the speed at that level. The size of the guys that had this speed was more amazing to me. When I saw a 250-pound linebacker running with the running back all the way down field, changing direction as quickly as I've ever seen, it was almost unreal to me. It seemed impossible, but once I got on the field and showed my speed and quickness, it was back to business for me. Sitting back on the sidelines watching these guys, the two things that amazed me on that first day were how the wide receivers caught the ball and how hard John Elway was throwing it. I thought, *My God! That man can throw that pill.*

Admittedly, it intimidated me a little. I wasn't known for my catching abilities. In my heart and soul, I was a running back, and after all my training prior to going into the NFL, my eight weeks of preparation for the NFL was catching footballs. Whether it was as a wide receiver or catching punts, those were things I hardly ever did at my previous levels, so I focused on them, but the wide receivers on my team were doing it at a level and a pace that intimidated me a great deal.

I struggled as a wide receiver during mini-camp. I was always catching the football with my body; I just had a tough time catching with my hands. The way these wide receivers caught the ball and the way John Elway was flinging it with such velocity, it was borderline dangerous. I recall doing a bunch of agility drills under the clock. Even though the veterans had to attend the mini-camp, they didn't have to participate in the agility drills, shuttle runs, or catching drills. Most of them just sat there and hazed all the rookies while we were doing it.

One of the drills I remember was the side shuttle run. I don't know how it was over at the other camps, but at the Broncos camp, everything was filmed, and every drill was timed and recorded. They had years' worth of records on shuttle runs, vertical jumps, and bench presses, just to name a few, and they compared our performance and sized us up against those records. The shuttle run is a drill designed to measure quickness. One of my major attributes was the ability to make defenders miss me; I was considered extremely quick. I always felt I was quicker than I was fast. It may sound a little crazy, but my quickness made me look faster.

I was the next-to-last rookie to go on this particular drill (the ten-yard shuttle run), and the coaches were there with their stopwatches. The veterans were there, too, watching us and getting a good laugh out of it. It was understandable because guys were slipping and falling on their butts, trying to start off too fast. These were drills I had been doing in my training regimens already because I was informed by my agents of the type of drills we would have to do. Plus, I did about sixty of those when the scouts came out to my college to work me out, so I had my fair share of practice with these particular agility drills.

The first time I performed the ten-yard shuttle run, I did really well, and the coaches did a double-take on the stopwatch. The strength and conditioning coach informed me that I had broken a Denver Broncos record in the shuttle run. That was a confidence booster for me because I had been labeled as the quickest and one of the fastest guys in camp.

The mini-camp wasn't bad and proved extremely beneficial to me in many ways. It was more or less roll call for the coaches to see what they had. I was getting a chance to meet the other players and learn the lay of the land. The veterans didn't participate that much, so it was a way for them to get to know the rookies they'd be working with and see what kind of talent was coming in. It was all mental for me—a time to get the starstruck out of my system and to get an idea of what the speed demands were going to be like. After that, training camp would be all business.

After mini-camp, I made the decision to stay in Denver and get some additional training and more used to the thin air. Most of the rookies stayed on because we all needed to get used to running in the high altitude. We did a lot of the forty-yard test. The first time I ran it, I didn't know what all it entailed. We had to do ten forty-yard yard sprints with thirty-five seconds of rest in between each, and we had to come in under a certain time every round. If you're not in good shape, the thin air in Denver can cause you to pass out, and after the seventh one of those forties, that's what I almost did. I'm embarrassed to admit that the first time I did the forty test, I couldn't complete it because the air was so thin and I couldn't catch my breath. I had to learn to pace myself and not start too fast. I stayed in Denver to work on it for about a month before I headed home to Staten Island.

When we reported to training camp, the first thing we had to do was that damn forty test. I was scared and nervous about it, even though I had been practicing it at home. Lucky for me, I continued to practice the test at home. I got each of my forties under the required time, and I didn't feel overly winded. That meant my body was getting acclimated to the thin air, and I was in great shape. Even though I was focused, I did notice that the tempo was even faster than it had been in mini-camp. I guess the business aspect of it kicked in, and everybody was looking for a job or wanting to keep the one they had. That meant everybody came in on point, and the speed was unbelievable.

I'm wearing Number 42 during Broncos' training camp.

A lot of armchair quarterbacks watch football on Sunday and Monday nights and don't realize what it entails to be a professional athlete, especially as a professional football player. Being part of a pro football team is a seven-a.m.-to-four-p.m. job, six days a week. It is simply nonstop, and we all worked our butts off. During the season, we reported to work at seven a.m. to begin weight lifting, and then we went to the classroom for a few hours to study film and go over plays. After that, we went out on the field and walked through all the plays we had gone over in the classroom before we broke for lunch. Then, it was right back into the classroom for a couple more hours, and then back to the field for practice for about an hour and forty-five minutes. Yes, it was only a total of an hour and forty-five minutes that we actually practiced, and everything else was done in the classroom, but that was during the season. Training camp was a whole different animal.

In training camp, we had two, sometimes three practices a day, and we spent most of our time on the football field trying to perfect the way we ran our plays. We did spend a couple of hours a day in the classroom during training, but our main thing during camp was the on-field work. Every single thing we did was taped; we couldn't get away with anything because everything was caught on film.

I remember my first professional football game. It's easy to remember that first game because it was against the Seattle Seahawks, and it was in Tokyo, Japan, on August 4, 1990—the American Bowl. The American Bowl had begun in 1986 when the NFL began scheduling games overseas during the preseason as a way to introduce the sport to different countries. I wore Number 42 because Payton's 34 was already taken by someone. Top-round draft picks could choose their own numbers, but as a rookie free agent from a small school and not even projected to make the final roster, I couldn't be too choosy. I was just happy they spelled my name right on the back of my jersey, and Number 42 wasn't bad.

I remember that whole monumental, long-ass trip. It was the longest I'd ever been on an airplane before, and I thought we would never land. I even got scared wondering how they could possibly have enough fuel in the plane to stay in the air that long. I was convinced we would crash and never make it to Tokyo alive. When I asked my teammates about my concerns, they had a good laugh at my expense, and in the end, we made it to Tokyo safe and sound. Once we landed, I felt like a rock star, because in Tokyo, they absolutely love American football. I can't recall signing as many autographs any other time. In Tokyo, there are a lot of people—I mean, a LOT—and they just love the sport. From the time we landed until the time we got to our hotel, it was an unbelievable experience that was way beyond anything I could have expected. There were no large crowds at Curtis High, and even at my Carson-Newman Championship Game, we only had 5,600 people in the stands. So, to get this type of attention was something I wasn't used to, and to be perfectly honest with you, it was something I really didn't like. It was even more shocking than the Southern hospitality I encountered in Tennessee.

I've always been a private person and kept to myself. I've always tried to fly under the radar and choose to stay out of the limelight. I never went looking to do an interview, but after I'd done everything I could to get out of it, I'd do one if I had to. Needless to say, the hordes of fans in Tokyo were a bit of a shock for me.

We arrived in Tokyo a week before the game, so we got a chance to do a little bit of sightseeing and get adjusted to the fifteen-hour time difference. I remember the first meeting we had when we all got together to discuss our game plan. In that meeting, we were told who was going to play in what quarter and with what group.

Before the game, I knew exactly when I was going to get in the game. They already had me projected as the first guy to go out as the punt returner, which was a good thing because kickoff return and punt return was the main position I would be hired for. They had already put me at the number one spot, and that was very encouraging.

Saturday was game day. We went into the locker room, got ourselves together, and got everything laid out for game day. It was all pretty amazing to me. When I walked in the locker room, they already had my uniform in my locker, along with everything else I needed. The decals on our helmets were on, a change from camp, when all we had on our helmets were our names. My helmet was shiny with a Denver Broncos decal on it, and I had this beautiful uniform sitting in my locker with my name stitched on the back of my jersey above the big Number 42. It was breathtaking for me, and I was tripping off that. It was game day, and everyone was all business. It was a far cry from what I was used to, and I really couldn't get over how we were catered to. The trainers, equipment men, and doctors were all at our disposal. Everything was available to us, and I felt like royalty. I felt like an NFL football player for the first time, and it was an awesome feeling to be donning the official orange, royal blue, and white.

Almost everyone had a ritual, even though I can't recall all of them. Some guys had to have their uniforms laid on the ground before putting them on. Some guys had to do certain things prior to games, whether it was going on the field and doing a work-out, listening to certain music on their Walkman, or eating certain things just before the game. Superstition is big at the professional level, and the people who have routines and rituals are certain their game will be screwed if they don't do it. It may seem ridiculous, but even I had a ritual.

My ritual was the same as it was in college. As soon as I got to the game field, I put my bags down, went out on the field, and walked around the whole field. I started in one corner of an end zone and walked 100 yards to the other end zone. Then, I walked along the back of the end zone and all the way down 100 yards to the other side of the end zone. I'd look up and say "Hi" to my mom and dad, and then I walked back in the locker room and started getting ready. I did that from my freshman year in college throughout my entire career in professional football; that was my ritual.

We all got ready for the game in our own way. When I got out there for pre-game warm-up, I said to myself, "Damn, this is your first pro football game." It was amazing to be there. It was about two hours before kickoff, and we had our 'specialty' guys go out first—the kickers, punters, kickoff, and punt return players. Two hours before kickoff, there were already at least 50,000 people in that stadium. It took my breath away.

We went through pre-game warm-ups and then back in the locker room to put on the rest of our equipment. About twenty minutes before kickoff, Coach Dan Reeves gave us our pre-game speech. It was the typical hoopla. "We want to execute. We want to do the things we've been practicing…" and so on and so forth. About ten minutes before kickoff, we went back out on the football field, fully armored this time. When I stepped through that tunnel, there must have been 80,000 people in the stands. I had never seen so many people in one building before. I could not believe what I was seeing, and I just kept gawking at the crowded stands with my jaw dropped in awe. Every seat was filled. It was such a rush and a great feeling.

I finally made my way to the sidelines. As they played the national anthem, I sat back and waited. I knew I had a fifty/fifty chance of getting on the field right away because I was on the first-string kick return team as well as the punt return team. The Seahawks got the ball first, and they drove the ball down the field on us and scored. Then, on kickoff return, they kicked away from me and right to the other kickoff return guy. We took the ball downfield and scored as well. On the next Seattle try, on fourth down, they ended up punting the ball.

It was my job to return that punt. I was on my own thirty-yard line, still in awe of all the people in the stands. I glanced up in the stadium, and I started to hear, "VT! VT!" That snapped me back to attention, and I quickly refocused myself. The punter let off a rocket of a punt. At the professional level, the rules are a little bit different. They can get away with a lot more at the pro level than they can in high school and college. Case in point, they punted the ball to me, and that ball was really up there. I thought for sure I was never going to be able to catch it. I started waving my hand over my head for a fair catch (telling everyone I had no intention of running with the ball and that I just wanted to secure the catch without the worry of getting blasted by a defender).

I focused and kept my eye on the ball the way I was taught. While the ball was in the air, I literally heard the opponents cursing me out. They were really trying to piss me off, calling my family names, and calling my momma names, and even calling my daddy names. They were doing anything they could to distract me from catching that ball, just as I'm sure they were trained to do. By the grace of God, I caught that football, but when I caught it, I looked at the referee and said, "Are you kidding me?"

The referee smiled and said, "Son, welcome to the NFL."

I just shook my head and handed him the ball. That was one heck of an experience in my first time ever touching a ball in an NFL game.

I think I had a return for about nine or ten yards that game. I really didn't get much playtime in that first game. It wasn't anything to write home about, but I didn't make any major mistakes either. I survived the first preseason game. Even though it was important that I did well in the preseason games, it was just as important that I did well in the training camp practices. I didn't get the chance to play much in the game, so my evaluation would come more from training camp. After the game, we flew back home and headed right back to training camp.

Once again, we were in practice mode, catching tons of footballs and punts. I was really focused on improving my punt return and wide receiver catching abilities. It was really crucial that I worked on my catching, especially playing with the Denver Broncos. We started by running routes before practice to get the quarterbacks warmed up, and that warmed us up as well. I had a problem catching the ball with my hands, and I was letting the ball reach my body. The receiver coach warned me, "That's a NO-NO!" but I wasn't the only rookie wide receiver that was not catching with their hands. There were several other culprits, and we used to get yelled at every day about catching with our bodies. We were not supposed to let the ball hit our chests, period. Between the coaches and quarterbacks, they got on us and they stayed on us. We got cussed out so many times about it that I lost count.

One particular practice, I was fourth or fifth in the pass catching line. We ran a route and then caught the ball with our bodies. Like always, the coach cussed us out and threatened to cut us if we continued to do it like that. I don't know if John Elway did it on purpose or not. He had some major velocity on his ball and changed the route from a quick hitch route (five-yard turnaround) to a hook route (twelve yards and then turn around). A twelve-yard hook route with John as the quarterback was not an easy thing to accomplish because he threw that ball so hard it whistled. I believe he did it on purpose to force us to catch with our hands, but once he threw the ball so hard that he hit the receiver right in the sternum, and I believe it cracked. I can't say for sure if John did that on purpose, but the timing of it was too coincidental considering we had just been yelled at for not using our hands to catch the ball. That poor receiver was done for the rest of camp. He was placed on injury reserve, but it guaranteed him an automatic spot on the team for the year on the injured reserve list.

I was next in line, and I had already gotten the memo from the last guy, so I attempted to catch with my hands. I dropped so many balls, but I never attempted to catch with my body again. Lesson learned, Mr. Elway, and I wanted to keep my sternum intact. During the course of training camp, my pass catching ability got better because of that, and my hands got stronger. The more catches I made, the more confident I got. My hands weren't exactly strong enough to catch balls from the John Elways of the world yet, but I was trying. I started doing fingertip push-ups in my room every night. My hands got stronger, and my catching ability got better.

The second preseason game we flew to Miami to play against the Miami Dolphins. I consider that game to be my breakout game. I had some really good kickoff returns and a great punt return. I really displayed my running ability, and I was going against one of the best punters in the national football league, Miami Dolphins' Reggie Roby. Reggie, like Ray Guy of the Oakland Raiders, stands out in my memory as one of the greatest punters I faced during my professional career. He was a unique punter in that he was a huge man, about six-four and 260 pounds, with unbelievable flexibility. When he punted the ball, his knee would touch his facemask after his follow-through, and the football would hang in the air seemingly forever.

The disadvantage for Reggie was that he would often outkick the coverage. He would not only kick it high, but deep, which gave the punt return man the opportunity to catch and run with the ball. Usually, the ideal punt is to kick the ball high and give the cover team a chance to tackle the punt returner. If your punter is outkicking the coverage and kicking it too far and high, then the return man has plenty of time to catch the ball with nobody in his face. Ray Guy would out-punt his coverage team as well, but nevertheless, these were two future Hall of Famers.

Reggie Roby gave me some really good balls to return, and that was the first time the coaches were able to see what I was capable of doing in a game situation. I was able to make it through the first round of cuts. The 'Turk' was the guy that knocked on your door during cutting time like some kind of NFL Grim Reaper. He was the one that informed the players the coach wanted to see them and always reminded them to bring their playbooks. I was always terrified that the Turk was coming for me, even though I knew I was having a good camp. At that actual moment of cuts, I couldn't help thinking I might be next. During that process, like everyone else, I'd just sit on the side of the bed and listen as the Turk knocked on doors and said, "Grab your playbook. Coach wants to see you," hoping the whole time that he wouldn't knock on my door. It was truly the worst, most helpless feeling in the world. Fortunately, I made it through that sweep of cuts.

The next preseason game was against the Indianapolis Colts. Prior to that game, if I can recollect correctly, Coach Dan Reeves had some type of health issue, a medical problem that forced him to go to the hospital and stay overnight. That game, he didn't travel with us.

I didn't have a good game against Indianapolis that year. In fact, on one of the punt returns, I dropped the ball, but I immediately recovered it. I was scared because the one thing I couldn't do as a rookie was drop punts or kicks, so I was glad I at least recovered the ball. As bad as my performance was, all things considered, I actually had a couple of okay runbacks in that game, but I could only focus on the mistakes I made. I couldn't afford to make any mistakes, and I had zero room for errors. I'll never forget when Dan Reeves came back to practice. He came over to me, and I said, "How are you doing, Coach?"

He answered, "I'm doing fine... That punt almost got away from you, huh?" He wasn't at the game, but he always watched film, and he watched it closely just like all of the Broncos coaches did; they were all about keeping records. It kind of surprised me that he would make that comment to me about the dropped punt, but he was the head coach, and he had to be on top of his game as well.

I said, "Yeah, Coach, but you saw I jumped on it right away."

"Oh, yeah, you jumped on that ball. That's good. That's real good."

I will never forget that awkward conversation.

The next wave of cuts came up that week, and I was a little bit more concerned this time because I dropped that ball, but the Turk never knocked for me. I was still slated (in pencil, anyway) as the number one punt returner for the team. So, things looked pretty decent for me with one more preseason game to go.

I knew there was some concern about the wide receiver slots. Ricky Nattiel hadn't had any breakout games during the preseason so far, and I knew there were talks that they were trying to decide whether to keep me or Ricky. I believe it was between the two of us, and one of us had to go.

Ricky had a leg injury, and he wasn't going through full practices during training camp until that last week. He went through a whole week of full practice, and he looked pretty good. The word got out that he had to have a good showing in the last preseason game, or they were going to make a decision to keep me and let him go. So, that whole week, Ricky busted his butt. He stayed in every drill and did all the things he had to do to make sure he got an opportunity to play that last preseason game.

I knew this was a make-it-or-break-it for me, and I think that alone was just too much pressure, because the first punt return, I ended up dropping the ball, and the other team recovered it. I was so nervous that I was literally sick to my stomach, and later during the course of the game, when they had me on offense, I ran a down out and up. I was wide open… and I dropped the ball. I was just mentally self-destructing. I was pushing myself too much, terrified of getting cut, and making mistake after mistake. And, as my luck would have it, that was Ricky Nattiel's breakout game. He caught five or six balls for 100-plus yards and a touchdown. Ricky did what he had to do, and I had the game from hell.

Coach Reeves spoke to the team after the game. He said, "You guys really work your butts off during training camp, but the last cuts are coming tomorrow, and we're going to have to make some really tough decisions." Truth be told, it wasn't looking too good for me.

That next day, I didn't have a good feeling about my chances. In fact, I had already packed my things because I was sure that under the circumstances, I was heading home. I didn't feel very confident about making the team. As I expected, I got that knock on the door.

"Grab your playbook," said the Turk. "Coach wants to see you."

I went into Coach Dan Reeves's office, and he sat me down and said, "Vernon, you had a great camp, and you're going to have a fine career in this league, but unfortunately it won't be with the Denver Broncos. You struggled at the end, and what we really need now is some experience. We're going to keep Ricky, and there are talks of having a practice squad team. We should know something within the next few days, and if we do, we want to bring you back and put you on the practice squad.

"Practice squad is a developmental group of guys that are on the team, just not on the forty-seven-man roster. You'll practice with the team and travel if the team wants you to, but you won't dress for the games and won't earn the full salary. The practice squad is paid a developmental player salary, which is really not that much, but at least you'd still be a part of the team."

He could tell I was really disappointed about it as he went on. "I know you feel bad now, Vernon, but you'll be alright. You're going to have a career in this league because you can play this game. You're going to do well in this league, so you just hang in there."

I stood up and shook his hand and said, "Coach, thank you for the opportunity, and I wish I could have made it with the Broncos, but I guess it's not in the cards."

"You keep your head up," he told me.

I walked out, got my things, and was escorted to the airport.

My rookie year with the Buffalo Bills.

Chapter 27:
Signing with the Buffalo Bills

Icalled Coach Olivieri and said, "Look, I want to let you know before it hits the newspaper wire that I just got re-leased. If you can pick me up at the airport, I'd appreciate it."

He said, "I'll be there."

It was probably the shortest plane ride ever because I did not want to take that trip back home to New York. I did a lot of think-ing during the flight. I felt like I had blown a golden opportunity, and I was disappointed in myself. I was sure the other NFL teams would look at that last preseason game and see how bad I played. I kept thinking that no one was going to give me another shot. I kept saying to myself, "All I need is one more shot. I know what I did wrong. I lost my focus. My family needs this. Please, God, I need one more shot."

When I got off that plane and went down to baggage claim at the bottom of the escalator, there were several coaches and a few of my former teammates from high school. Coach Olivieri was among them. I looked at him, and the first and only thing I said to him was, "It's not over, Coach. This thing isn't over." We got in a car, and it was a quiet drive—a really quiet drive. I didn't say anything.

During the drive, I got a phone call from my agents. Tony said, "Hey, V, you're not going to be relaxing for too long, buddy. You're flying out tomorrow morning, and if things work out the way I know they are, you're going to end up signing with Buffalo Bills. They wanted you right after the draft, but it just didn't seem like it was going to be a good fit at the time. But now, they've created their practice squad, and they want to sign you on."

Denver also called for me to join their practice squad, but I had already decided I wanted to be in Buffalo. The very next day, I flew out to Buffalo and met the coaches. They wanted to confirm what they had seen prior to Draft Day, so I ran the forty-yard dash again. Evidently, I did well, because they immediately signed me on their practice squad. I was officially a member of the Buffalo Bills Practice Squad for 1990.

It was a special time for me and my family. To be honest, it still hadn't hit me that I was officially a member of a professional football team. I was now really a part of the NFL. I didn't think much of it because I wasn't playing in any of the games; I was just so happy to get another shot. God blessed me with another opportunity, and I had every intention of taking full advantage of it. Signing with the Bills was extra special because it enabled me to reunite with one of my college teammates, Brent Collins. The Bills drafted him in the seventh round that year. Brent was an outstanding linebacker in college, and he was a pretty cool guy.

I remember walking into the locker room for the first time and realizing guys like Andre Reed, Bruce Smith, Thurman Thomas, Darryl Talley, Carlton Bailey, Jim Kelly, James Lofton, Don Beebe, and Steve Tasker were now my teammates. It was an amazing opportunity for me to be a part of that team, learning from the best. What more could I ask for?

About three weeks after I joined up with the Bills, another one of my former college teammates, David Pool, signed with them. He had been drafted in the sixth round by the Chargers the same year I came out. I don't know what happened in San Diego, but a few weeks into the season, they released him, and the Bills wasted no time in signing him. It was awesome having David and Brent on the team because I had someone familiar to hang with, not to mention they were some really cool cats.

Being on the practice squad was extremely difficult for me because I was (and still am) a competitor and it was tough practicing week after week without playing a game. I just kept saying to myself, "If I keep doing my thing at practice, they won't have any choice but to activate me," but week after week, I was disappointed. I was grateful for being where I was, but I was extremely hungry for more; I was improving every day, and my confidence was growing during each practice. In fact, the defensive starters used to get mad at me quite often because I went full speed all the time. It didn't matter where we were on the field or what we were doing, I finished every single play in the end zone. A couple of defensive backs said, "Damn, VT, slow your ass down," and I would answer, "Why don't you just speed your ass up? This is my Sunday, and I'm not slowing down for nobody!"

I knew the coaches were aware of what I was doing at practice. I think they kind of enjoyed watching the defense get mad at me. They liked the fact that I made them work, and I think they liked the way I competed, but when it actually counted, I didn't get the chance to suit up and compete on Sundays. That was extremely difficult for me to swallow each week, but I did not let that deter me from doing my best whenever I was on the field. I had good people in my corner to keep me sane and keep my mind right, and that was something else I was thankful for.

A salary for a practice squad player wasn't much compared to an active player's salary. When I signed my first NFL contract with the Denver Broncos, they gave me a $5,000 signing bonus, and after taxes, it came up to maybe $3,800, of which $3,000 went right home to my aunt to help her take care of my brothers and sisters. So, when I got released by the Denver Broncos, I got extremely scared, wondering where I was going to get my money from to support my family. When I received that phone call from my agent informing me that Buffalo wanted to sign me, I felt like a huge weight was lifted off my shoulders. I had steady money coming in, about $5,500 a week. It was nowhere near what those other guys on the team were making, but it was more than enough to support my family back home.

I was still living like I was in college. Most of my money went back home to help with the bills, and I was living on ramen noodles and Kool-aid during my rookie year, but that was okay because they did feed us during practice. I had enough money to take care of my rent, but my main thing was sending money home. My family came first.

Often, my competitive edge and my instinct as an athlete would kick in, and I didn't want to settle for the practice squad. At those times, I called Coach Olivieri, and he would give me reassurance and encouragement. I also got calls from my assistant football coach, Bob McGhie, telling me to hang in there, as well as calls from my agents. Evidently, they had a good relationship with the front office people, so they periodically checked in to see how I was doing.

The more weeks that went by, the more intense practice got for me. I competed so hard that the veterans had to tell me to cool it and slow down because I was making them look bad. The more time that went by, the less I cared what my teammates thought about me and what I was doing on the field. I would flat-out tell them, "Hey, you got a job. You're playing on Sundays. I'm going to do my thing. You hate me all you want. I don't care. I'm going to do my thing."

Not all the veterans hated on my practice regimen. One particular practice, it was snowing, which was very common during that time of the year, about the eleventh or twelfth week into the season. Like I said before, practice was my Sunday; those practices were my games. I got after it pretty hard, and there were some veterans that thrived on that. One of the defensive backs said, "Hey, V, you keep doing what you're doing, man. You're making us better by the way you're running your routes, running full speed on every play! You're forcing me to stay on top of my game!"

I got a great deal of respect, and at that point, they started rooting for me to actually get off the practice squad. Honestly, I had a lot of really good practices. My agent called in for progress reports, and he was informed that I was one of the hardest workers on the team and that I was really fighting to get a spot on the active roster. They said, "His work ethic is off the charts. We love him!" That was the response Tony and Howard got from the Buffalo Bills' front office. Tony called me and informed me, "Hey, you're doing well out there. You keep up the good work. This is what they're saying about you."

That made me feel good and work even harder—if that was even possible.

Chapter 28:
The Tale of the Missing Mazda

I really liked sports cars when I was younger, and I had always wanted one, so once I had the funds, I went out and purchased a brand new 1990 Mazda RX7, a beautiful little sports car. We didn't have any hard weather at the time, and everybody was still driving little cars around Buffalo. I was really digging that Mazda RX7.

Around the tenth game of the season, there were reports of a snowstorm coming to Buffalo. I remember it was a Monday because we worked out in the weight room, watched film, and then did a walkthrough in our mini-dome. Prior to the storm hitting, we did all of our stuff in the indoor facility, and it was during that time that the storm hit. Our practice ended at about two p.m. that afternoon. I did my normal routine after practice. I showered, grabbed my bag and my coat, and headed out the door to the parking lot, which was buried in snow. I walked to where my car was parked, but it wasn't there! "You've got to be freaking kidding me!" I said. "How in the hell did they steal a car off the damn Buffalo Bills complex?" I immediately rushed back to receptionist's desk in the main office.

"Look," I said, "call the authorities. My car's been stolen."

The receptionist said, "What? You've got to be kidding." She couldn't believe it because we had such stringent security. "No way, VT. Your car couldn't be stolen."

"My car isn't out there where I parked it."

While I was reporting this emergency to the receptionist, Darryl Talley (one of our linebackers) passed me and overheard us. He said, "V, what's going on, man?"

"D, my car is gone, man. They stole my car."

He said, "No way, man. Where did you park it?"

I walked outside with him and pointed because I could see the space from where we were in the building. "I parked right there."

He looked at me and looked over there and started laughing. It pissed me off. Darryl Talley was a big dude, and I was trying to figure out how I was going to get this big dude down and beat his ass. He just kept laughing about my car being stolen and I still had a lot of New York mentality in me. "What the hell is so funny, man?" I asked him.

"V," he said, "come over here, man."

We walked over to where my car had been parked. He took his hand and basically rubbed the snow off my car. The snow plow guy had come and piled snow completely over my Mazda! "V, look around. Do you see all these cars that have flags on their antennas? This is why... so they can find their cars. It's alright, man. I won't tell."

The next day, all sorts of jokes were thrown out about me losing my car. Thurman Thomas said, "Hey, V, where did you lose your car, man? You found it underneath that damn snow, huh? I bet you don't lose that car now! Wanting a damn sports car in Buffalo. What the hell is wrong with you?"

I heard it all, and forty-eight hours later, I traded that RX7 in for a Nissan Pathfinder. Yeah, I officially became a truck man.

Chapter 29:
My Teammates in Buffalo

Marv Levy, a brilliant man, knew the game inside and out. He was pretty laid back, not a yeller or a screamer. He was one of those guys you just had to like because of his demeanor and the way he interacted with the players. He was a small man, about five-nine and 160 pounds soaking wet.

Every team has one of those guys—I guess you would call him a teacher's pet, a favorite. Thurman Thomas was the coach's pet. It was no secret, and we called him the spoiled brat of the family because Thurman got whatever he wanted whenever he wanted it. We started using that to our advantage, and if we ever wanted anything—like cutting practice short or practicing indoors—we would go to Thurman first and have Thurman get on Marv to get whatever we wanted.

A perfect example was one Friday practice prior to a Monday night game. We went in the locker room, and all the guys started saying, "Damn. We don't need to be out here all damn day. We can cut the workout short and cut the film time short because we've already gone over it, and we can get out of practice early. We can literally get out of here by one."

We would usually stay until about three thirty, so we got the brilliant idea to get Thurman Thomas to get on Marv Levy to get us out of practice early that day. Thurman had a unique way of getting what he wanted from Marv. Basically, Thurman would throw miniature tantrums. We told Thurman the game plan and he agreed. It all started right then and there in the locker room. As soon as we gave him the game plan, he put it into effect and immediately started complaining, "Damn, Marv! Why the hell we got to be out here all damn day for? We got the game on Monday. We don't have to be out here all freaking damn day, Marv."

Marv would often come into the locker room to interact with us, and every time he did, Thurman complained to him like he was really pissed off, even though it was all an act. Thurman Thomas was a football genius, but he was also a damn good actor.

When we got onto the practice field and start stretching, all we could hear was Thurman pitching to get out of practice. "Marv, I can't believe you're doing this. Watch, you're going to lose your damn job if any one of us gets hurt. Freaking Marv. Get us the hell out of here, freaking Marv."

We were trying not to laugh, but it was just too funny. We just made sure Marv didn't see us laughing, but the more Thurman talked, the more serious Thurman got, and the more Marv Levy had to listen to him. Finally, Marv had enough of Thurman and said in his characteristic nasal voice, "Alright, guys, we'll get out of here about one. Thurman wants to go home."

We all started laughing. That was just part of being a big family, and that's exactly what we were.

The one person out of everyone that I was really close to on the Buffalo Bills was James Lofton. I was one guy that really wasn't hazed because James Lofton didn't allow it. I don't know what it was, but James actually took a liking to me and took me under his wing. The only thing I had to do before and after every practice for the whole year was carry his equipment. After practice, he took off his equipment and handed it to me, and I took it and put it back in his locker. In return, no one could bother me or haze me, and it was something I really didn't mind. I had a future Hall of Famer who actually liked me, and I looked up to him big time. Hell, carrying his equipment worked out to be a pretty good deal for me.

Jim Kelly was one of the best quarterbacks I ever had the pleasure of playing with. Everyone knew of our offense—the infamous no-huddle. We made it famous over in Buffalo. We basically did everything from the line of scrimmage, and we lit it up. Jim was a fierce competitor, one of the toughest guys I've ever met. He took some hits so hard that afterwards, I didn't know how in the world he got up and kept trucking. Jim wasn't a small guy. He was about six-four, 230 pounds. He was a street quarterback. If he didn't get the plays from the sideline for whatever reason, or if it didn't get through the microphone into his helmet, he would damn near write plays on the grass, telling guys where to run, and I'll be damned if it didn't work. Jim didn't have to say anything; it was his actions that brought out the high level of play in everyone else. He was just one of those quarterbacks that wanted to win at any cost. He did whatever he had to do to get the job done. That was the kind of offense tailor made for Jim Kelly.

Not only was Jim a great leader on the football field, but he was one of the most down-to-earth guys I have ever met. He didn't act like he was better than everyone else (even though he was better than most). He gave the same respect to everyone he came in contact with. In fact, Jim and I got along extremely well. We hung out outside of football a few times, and there is only one word I can use to describe Jim Kelly: genuine!

There is one particular story about Jim that I'll never forget. Jim, at the time, was one of the highest-paid players in the National Football League, and I was probably the lowest-paid player in the NFL. We got paid every Monday, and we had to pick up our checks or check stubs up in the main office. Rich Stadium housed our Accounting, Payroll, and Human Resources Departments, so when we had to take care of any type of administrative stuff, we went to the offices above the stadium. This one particular Monday, I went upstairs to grab my check, and Jim Kelly was already upstairs to get his.

We got to talking, and we agreed that later on that night, we were going to go meet up for drinks and food. As we were riding down in the elevator, I said, "Jimbo, let me see your check, man. I want to see how much you make."

He said, "No, bro. I can't let you see that."

I pleaded, "Come on, dude. Let me see."

He handed me his check. I'm not going to put his business out in the street, but let's just say his week's pay was enough to buy an entire house—a really nice house in a great neighborhood. I looked at his check and I looked at him, and when the elevator doors opened, I looked at him again. His check stub looked like an actual check, and as soon as the elevator doors opened, I immediately bolted out of the elevator with it in my hands.

At Rich Stadium, you get off the elevator, go through the tunnel, and go into the stadium, and it's wide open. I started sprinting with what I thought was Jim Kelly's check. I ran all the way across the other side of the stadium to the other side of the end zone, rubbing it all over me and taunting, "You want this back, Jimbo?"

He said, "It's only a check stub, bro," and we started cracking up.

I don't think I will ever in my lifetime see that amount of money on one weekly check stub ever again. It was an astronomical amount of money, but looking back at everything he did for that franchise, he deserved every penny of it. That was a Jim Kelly moment I will never forget.

Back at home, everything was fine. I was continuously sending money to my aunt, and everything seemed to be okay. It was a really exciting time for me and for my family at the beginning of my rookie year, when I actually signed with the Buffalo Bills. I literally cried like a baby because I knew I would have money coming in—not because I made the football team and not because it was my childhood dream, but because I was finally able to support my family. We were able to keep our house, and all of my brothers and sisters were able to stay together under one roof. That was the only thing going through my mind because I had to keep everyone together, and now the Bills were helping me to do just that—even if my check paled in comparison to the great Jim Kelly's.

VT and Jim Kelly during Super Bowl week.

Chapter 30:
Getting Activated

The Buffalo Bills lit it up in 1990. We were winning, game in and game out. By week twelve, we had already clinched a playoff spot. What we were working on next was home-field advantage throughout the entire playoffs, so we had to win at least two of the last three games.

The season was going extremely well. We had already locked ourselves in the playoffs, and we were heading into our last three games. We won the first game. During the second game, an away game, one of our key wide receivers, Don Beebe, broke his leg. Clarkston Hines and I were sitting there watching the game in my apartment. He was another wide receiver out of Duke that was on the practice squad with me. Thurman Thomas was running the ball, and Don Beebe was trying to block for him. I believe Thurman and the defensive back rolled up onto Don Beebe's leg, and it snapped in two. As soon as that happened, they immediately had the ambulance come out and get him. We were sitting there watching, just sitting there looking at one another. Clarkston said, "You know you're getting activated."

I said, "Dude, you can get activated just as quickly as I can. It's one of us."

"Yeah it's one of us, but it's you. I'm not stupid, man. I see how things are in practice. You're doing great at practice, man. It's going to be you, bro. You're going to be activated in the playoffs. Can you believe that, dude?"

I know it was kind of pitiful on our part for thinking this way at someone else's expense, and I apologized to God afterwards, but then we started talking about money because there was a big difference from the flat salary of the practice squad and the contract of the active players. We wanted to get on the active roster before the playoffs.

We lost Don Beebe for the rest of the year, but thank goodness we won that second game. The last game of the season was against the Washington Redskins, and that Monday when I went to work,

I got pulled into Marv Levy's office. Marv informed me he was going to activate me. I guess I was speechless because I just looked at him at first, at a loss for words. All I could utter was, "Thanks."

Coach Levy said, "Don't thank me. You've earned it."

I had a big smile on my face when I walked out. I immediately called Coach Fred and told him I was going to be on the active roster and was going to play against the Washington Redskins. I also called my family. I was ecstatic. I was actually going to be a part of the game plan.

It wouldn't be much of a game for me, as I was only going to be doing kickoff cover and maybe a few kickoff returns, but we had a kickoff returner in Don Smith and a punt returner in Al Edwards. Al was a really good buddy of mine at the time. They called us twins because we were almost the same size. I think I was a little bit taller than Al, but I didn't say anything. I can't take anything away from Al. He was a solid return man and a good wide receiver.

We prepared all during the week to play, and then we headed out to Washington. Some of my people were there from Staten Island, and it was awesome that some of my old coaches and other players came to support me. I only got a handful of plays in and didn't really get a chance to touch the ball at all. I didn't do any kickoff or punt returns, so I really couldn't show what I could do, which was unfortunate.

That following Monday, Marv Levy pulled me in the office and said, "V, we really need experience on the active roster, and right now, you just don't have that experience. We're going to have to deactivate you."

I didn't know what that meant. "I'm getting cut?" I asked.

"No, no, no. You're still on the team, and your pay won't be affected. We're just not going to activate you for the entire playoffs."

I said, "I can't play in the playoffs? If we go to the Super Bowl, can I play in that?"

He said, "No, no. Once we deactivate you before the playoffs, you have to be deactivated for the rest of the season."

I was really disappointed, but he gave me words of encouragement.

"You have such a bright future. You're going to be just fine. Right now, I've got to do what's best for the football team, and we have to get experience out on the football field. This is the best move for the football team."

I was pretty disappointed, but what could I do? I said, "That's alright, Coach. You have to do what you have to do. I understand." So, I was deactivated for the remainder of the season, and that was a crushing blow to me because all I was thinking about was playing in the Super Bowl, and that dream was crushed right there in Coach Levy's office.

At this point, we had home field throughout all the playoffs, so both playoff games were played at home. We had a bye week the first week, and then we had two games to win to go to the Super Bowl. First, we beat Miami, and then we played against the Los Angeles Raiders. The weather was horrendous, cold, and snowy, but we had to win that game to go to the Super Bowl. We beat the snot out of those poor Raiders, as all they wanted to do was get out of the snow. They did not want any part of that game, and we ended up winning big, beating them fifty-one to three. After that, the Bills were on their way to the Super Bowl to face our neighbors, the New York Giants.

Our rookie season with the Buffalo Bills.
David Pool and I enjoying Super Bowl weekend.

Chapter 31:
Super Bowl XXV (1990)

It was the Buffalo Bills vs. the New York Giants in Super Bowl XXV. That year, the Super Bowl was in Tampa, Florida, and it was beautiful down there, absolutely gorgeous. We practiced at the Tampa Bay Buccaneers facility, and it was much needed, because we were in snow out in Buffalo. It wasn't all that sunny when we first got to Florida. It was cloudy, but warm, and boy did we enjoy ourselves! Every movie star and sports celebrity and political figure you can think of was in Tampa. The whole ambience of the Super Bowl was overwhelming, from the press conferences to practices. There were media galore and interviews out the wah-zoo. I was just a peon, but I did practice with the team and did everything everyone else did other than playing the game. It was an experience unlike anything I've ever been a part of.

The actual Super Bowl night, I went out on the football field to a packed house with the lights glittering and cameras flashing. There were VIPs and Hollywood royalty everywhere, and it was fantastic. I even got a hug from Whitney Houston herself! All she knew was that I was a football player, and she gave me love. I reached out to hug her, and she hugged me back. She was absolutely gorgeous, and what a sweet lady she was. She stole the show when she sang the national anthem, and if there was one dry eye in that whole stadium, I would have been surprised. Whitney's rendition of "The Star-Spangled Banner" was memorable, truly heartfelt. It was literally the most beautiful thing I've ever heard. She did our country justice, she did the Super Bowl justice, and she did herself justice, and that was one hell of a moment!

The game went back and forth. We were playing against the New York Giants, and David Meggett was putting on a show. He had a fantastic game; in fact, I thought he was going to win the MVP. I remember there being under two minutes left in the game. The Giants had the lead, and we got in our no-huddle mode in high-tempo fashion. Jim Kelly, Thurman Thomas, James Lofton, and Andre Reed all went to work. Man, they moved that ball downfield! It was just poetry in motion, and it was going down to the seconds. The last play before attempting the field goal was a screen play to Thurman Thomas. Thurman got it up to the thirty-something yard line, leaving Scott Norwood to face a forty-seven-yard field goal kick to win the game. By this time, there were about eight seconds left on the clock. Jim Kelly had had a beautiful drive going downfield. We started on our twenty, and now it was up to Scott, who was having a really good year kicking.

The people on the Bills sidelines were all holding hands and breath, gathering together. I looked at David Pool and said "Man, we're about to get a Super Bowl ring! He's not going to miss this."

Then David said, "Yeah, man, we're getting a ring."

We were all holding hands as the holder took the snap. Placement looked pretty good, and Scott Norwood booted the ball. He had plenty of distance, so we got excited. From our angle, it looked like the ball went through the goal posts, but when we looked across the field and saw the New York Giants celebrating, we knew Scott's kick had not hit the mark, and it was no good.

We were still in disbelief; we couldn't believe he missed that field goal. I just stood there and helplessly watched the Giants celebrate and Bill Parcells get lifted up. Bill was pretty big, so I don't know how the hell they lifted his big ass up, but they managed.

We worked our way back into the locker room, and Scott was there sitting by himself, looking defeated. I went up to him and patted him on his shoulder pad, but he never looked up. I really felt bad for him because once the media was clear to come in the locker room, they swarmed him. I knew that was probably the worst feeling any professional athlete could ever have.

That Super Bowl, again, was one of my most memorable experiences—something I will always cherish, even though I didn't get to play and we lost by just one point, nineteen to twenty, in a game where both teams played so well that not one turnover happened on either side.

Coach Olivieri, his wife, Joan, and I at a Curtis H.S. football dinner. I gave my Super Bowl jersey to my H.S.

To have the opportunity my rookie year to attend the Super Bowl was an amazing experience, but I couldn't help thinking about missing out on getting a Super Bowl ring; little did I know that even losers are presented with one just for being there. They don't like calling it a 'loser's ring' or a 'consolation ring.' They call it an AFC or NFC Championship Ring, depending on which conference the losing team is in. The winner's ring is bigger and blingier, of course.

A few days later, the city of Buffalo held a parade for us, and the mayor congratulated us on a great season. To be honest, all I heard out of his mouth was "blah, blah, blah…" and I'm sure I wasn't the only player or coach hearing the same damn thing. I know the mayor had to be politically correct, but we had just lost the Super Bowl by one lousy point in the last seconds of the game, and no one was in the mood to hear a pep talk.

Shortly after our last team meeting, I went home to New York to spend some time with my family. I stayed at home for about a month, and then I went back to Buffalo to train in the off-season. I was determined to never be on a practice squad again, so I went back to Buffalo and started training hard, getting myself ready for the following season.

I lived in Buffalo throughout the off-season since it was important that I conduct my training there. The coaches stayed there as well. They went on vacation and did their thing, but for the most part, there were always at least some coaches there. It was a great opportunity to get some major assistance during my stay. I wasn't the only one to stick around; we had a couple of the other first-year athletes that stayed to get additional training as well. What I wanted to focus on was catching as many punts as possible. The punter never stayed, though, and only came in from time to time and stick around town for a little bit, so I had to rely on a jugs machine. A jugs machine is a machine that kicks out footballs like a punt or a kick. It has two wheels spinning real fast, and you put the ball in between the wheels so it can shoot the ball out and up in the air, simulating a punt or a kick. I literally lived on the jugs machine that whole off-season, catching balls with one hand, catching balls with another ball in my hand, having the ball angled on one side of the field, and forcing myself to have to chase it down and catch it. I was determined to excel at that position.

Kickoff returns are different; you don't really have to work too much on those. You have plenty of time to catch it, and even if you drop it, you have plenty of time to pick it up and go. Punt returns are a different story. When the ball is punted, you HAVE to catch the ball. There are no ifs, ands, or buts about it, and you cannot let it drop. You have eleven guys, including linebackers, defensive backs, and even some linemen running down trying to take your head off while you're looking up in the air, trying to catch the ball. It's more difficult to catch punts than kicks for that reason, so what I focused on in the off-season was being a really good return man.

The issue wasn't me running the ball. I knew once I had the ball in my hands, it was over. It was just making sure I secured the catch and that I had the opportunity to make something happen. That was what I focused on. I was so focused and in tune on trying to get my skills elevated on punt returning that I had the Buffalo Bills media guy come out and record me catching punts.

The interesting part about that is that Marv Levy took a special interest in me catching punts in the off-season. He started helping me sometimes when I went out to practice. He came out there to watch and gave what little advice he had, and then together, we would go in the film room and critique my performance. It was funny because I wasn't use to a head coach taking such a special interest in helping me develop my skill.

One day, I was watching a film of me catching a bunch of punts, and I realized it was beautiful. It was really close up, and I was able to see exactly what I was doing. Marv pointed out one particular thing. "V," he said, "I noticed you never follow the ball through into your hands. Your helmet never moves. Why is that?"

It wasn't like I was dropping a whole bunch of footballs. In fact, I caught 98 percent of my balls. I said, "Well, Coach, I am moving my eyes. I'm looking the ball in with my eyes. I don't really like moving my head. I just shift my eyes down into my hands."

Marv said, "Oh, okay. I did not realize that." Instead of him pushing back and saying, "No, I want you to do it this way," he just let me be me. "If that's what works for you, that's fine. I never thought of that... Yeah, you are moving your eyes." After that, he left it alone, and I thought that was pretty interesting.

Chapter 32:
From First to Worst—Buffalo Bills to Los Angeles Rams (1991)

hen training camp came around, I was hyped. I felt I'd had a great off-season. I trained extremely hard and was physically and mentally prepared. There was no stopping me. To make a long story short, I took care of business in all four of the preseason games. I didn't leave any doubt in anyone's mind that VT was all business. Even Jim Kelly came up to me after the last preseason game and said, "Hey, VT, you're going to make this team. How could you not make the team?" I was getting kudos from the other veterans on the team as well, guys like Thurman Thomas, Andre Reed, and James Lofton. They felt confident that I was going to make the team, and I felt pretty confident about it as well because I had excelled.

By Sunday morning, the suspense was killing me. They weren't going to make the announcements until later that afternoon, but after we went in to work out, I went to see Nick, the wide receiver coach. "Coach," I said, "do you have word? The suspense is killing me."

At first, Nick answered, "Well, you know, you need to be patient." Then, after a minute, he told me, "You probably need to go and talk to Marv. It just didn't work out."

My jaw dropped. I could not believe it. I immediately went over to Marv Levy's office. If I'm not mistaken, Marv Levy and Bill Polian, the GM, were both there. "Marv, is it true? I'm not going to make it?"

"Well, V, you've had a great preseason. We're trying to slip somebody else in on a roster."

"I'm not going to make it?" I asked again, completely shocked.

He said, "We want you on this football team, but there are some other people we're afraid of losing. If we put them on the waiver wire, we're not going to get them back, so we made a decision to put you on waivers. We feel we're going to get you back, and then we're going to put you back on the active roster."

I looked at Marv and at Bill. "Guys, I'm not coming back," I said. "Honestly, I had a really good preseason. Somebody else is going to get me if you do this. I won't be back."

"Well, it's a move we have to make, and we feel confident we'll get you back. You'll be back."

I shook both their hands and left. They did put me on waivers; in other words, they released me. I went back to my apartment and pulled out my football magazines. I was trying to figure out which team was going to pick me up. I knew it was going to be someone, but unfortunately for me, the teams with the worst record from the previous year would have the first right of refusal in signing me. Less than two hours later, I get a phone call from my agents, and they informed me the Los Angeles Rams had picked me up off waivers, and I would be their starting kickoff and punt return man for the upcoming Sunday game. I immediately packed my bags, got everything together, and called my family members. My high school coach, Bob McGhie, got his van and grabbed my things from my apartment, and I was on the first plane to California.

As soon as my agent called and told me the Rams had picked me up, I immediately checked out their records and their status. It was then that I realized I was going from one of the best teams in the National Football League to one of the worst. Still, it was exciting to know I was going to be on the active roster and would be playing that very Sunday. Knowing that made my flight to California a pretty exciting one.

I got into California late that afternoon, went to the facilities, met the coaches, and got my locker, equipment, and everything I needed for the next day's practice. I can recall my first practice and the first time going in the locker room. I was greeted very warmly by Henry Ellard, Flipper Anderson, Aaron Cox, Robert Delpino, and Sam Lilly. A whole bunch of guys embraced me and made me feel at home, welcoming me instantly. Even Jim Everett, a well-known quarterback at the time, came over to greet me. It was a really good thing right out of the gate. They immediately put me on as a wide receiver and kickoff and punt return guy, so that's what I practiced for that whole week. I remember my first game with them was against the Arizona Cardinals. My first time touching the ball as a Ram, I returned a punt for twenty yards. I was trying to score every time I touched the ball. I was still a little pissed off at the Bills for letting me go, so I was playing with a big-time chip on my shoulders. I had a couple of other good runs, and then the bottom hit. I caught a punt and was making several moves to elude some defenders when one of them hit my arm, and I fumbled the ball.

On the next punt return, they 'squibbed' it (kicking the ball extremely low to where it the ball skipped along the ground several times before getting to me). I tried to pick it up off the ground, but the Cardinals defender timed it up and hit me just as I touched the ball. I lost the ball again, and the other team recovered it. The result? I had two fumble return losses in my first game with the Rams.

Our head coach at the time, John Robinson, was a passionate guy. He loved the game, and he was a player's coach. During that game, he had pulled me aside and said, "You're going to be okay. You'll be alright."

The following Monday in our team meeting, Coach Robinson said, "Look, we're all going to make mistakes. We've just got to learn from it." In front of the whole team, he also reassured me, "V, I'm not going to cut you, man. You're here to stay. I may eat your lunch and get on you, but I'm not going to cut you. You're my guy. You got big-time talent."

That alone put me at ease, and I was able to forget about that first-game fiasco, so I had a pretty good second year. I was their leading kickoff and punt return man, and I convinced them to put me in a backfield every once in a while in third-down situations. The Rams realized I was more of a scat back than a wide receiver, so they put me in the game plan coming out of the backfield as a running back. I had almost achieved my childhood dream, which was to play running back in the NFL.

Returning a kick in my very first game with the Rams.

Taking a hand-off from Jim Everett.

*Hall of famer, Jackie Slater, giving me
pointers on how to run faster.*

Chapter 33:
The Bo Jackson Story (Part 2)

It was 1991 before I got to make good on the promise I had made to Bo Jackson that I would be playing against him one day. Bo was with the Raiders at the time, and I was still with the Rams; I knew we were going to eventually play against them. When that game came, I made sure I shook Bo's hand during the pre-game warm-ups. I did not introduce myself but just said, "Good luck, Bo," shook his hand, and left. I didn't want him to know who I was right away; I wanted to wait until after the game. Bo was on injured reserve that year; he had a serious hip injury that ended up being the demise of his football career.

I had a pretty good game. I scored my first NFL touchdown against the Raiders off of a nineteen-yard pass from Jim Everett. I came out of the backfield and did an arrow route, which basically means faking going out to the flats and then cutting across the middle. I caught the ball and ran about fourteen yards before diving the last four or five yards in the end zone. After that, I had some pretty decent punt returns. Even though we lost the game in the end, it was a pretty exciting time for me.

I specifically searched for Bo Jackson at the end of that game. When I found him, I shook his hand and said, "Good game, Bo."

He said, "Good game," and shook my hand.

As he was pulling away, I held onto his hand and said, "Hey, don't you remember me?" I took off my helmet and asked again, "You don't remember me?"

He looked at me like he was trying to remember me.

I said, "Bo, you don't remember being a guest speaker at a Junior Heisman Award ceremony in New York and you presented the awards? You don't remember a young man coming over to you and saying, 'I don't want your autograph. I just want to shake your hand because I'll be playing against you or with you someday'?"

His eyes opened up like silver dollars, as if he had seen a ghost. He could not believe it.

I said with a smile, "Didn't I tell you I was going to play with or against you one day?"

I knew Bo was strong, but I didn't realize how strong he was until he grabbed me and gave me a huge hug. Hell, I thought he was going to break every rib in my body. He just kept looking at me and patting me on my shoulder pads. He was at a loss for words, speechless. That was a moment I will never, ever forget. I was able to actually do exactly what I told Bo I was going to do. You only see things like this in the movies, and to this day, I still get goose-bumps just thinking about it.

I wouldn't say I had a great second year with the Rams, but I had a pretty good year under the circumstances. We won maybe four or five ball games that year, and to be perfectly honest, we were really terrible as a team. I went from the Buffalo Bills—a team that knew how to win—to a team that didn't have a clue. The Rams' losing streak was something I wasn't used to. I was used to winning. The Rams' whole mindset was totally jacked up. They were looking to lose because that's what they were used to. They had a here-we-go-again attitude. We could have had a fourteen-point lead in the game, but they still expected to lose their lead and lose the game. Being the competitor that I am, I was extremely frustrated about that. Evidently, by the end of the season, management got upset about it, too, and they ended up firing John Robinson and hiring Chuck Knox as head coach the following year.

This was a game against the Raiders.
I was trying to put on a show for Bo Jackson.

Chapter 34:
The Big-Hit—Rams vs. Bills

Rams Offensive Coordinator, Ernie Zampese, thought I had some potential to be an impact player for the team. Like always in the off-season, I worked like crazy, busting my butt. I spent half the time in the off-season out there in Anaheim to get myself prepared. I changed my number from 82 to 30 because I was told I was going to get a lot more backfield play. Number 34 was already taken, so 30 was the next best thing to having Payton's number—not to mention 30 looked good on me. The 1992 preseason came, and I lit it up in training camp.

I had already checked the schedule, and I knew we'd be playing my old team, the Buffalo Bills, on opening day. We went through the preseason, and I was never in fear for my job. I'd built up way too much confidence, and I was at that point in my career where I proved to be an impact player throughout the league. That whole week of preparing for the opening game, the final cuts were made, but I wasn't worried anymore about making the team.

I was just getting ready for those Bills on opening day. I don't think I've ever been more vocal in preparing for a football game than I was for that particular game, especially with the special teams. I knew those guys in Buffalo because I had played with them. I knew what they were all about. Another thing I knew about was their special teams, especially a great deal about Steve Tasker.

I knew Steve Tasker's M.O. He was by far one of the best special team's player I have ever had the pleasure of playing with or against. I had much love and respect for the guy because the son of a bitch never quit. He got after it and went a hundred miles an hour from start to finish, and that's what made him so exceptional. Preparing for the game, I had to let my new teammates know about Steve, I said, "Look, you can single block the one guy on our left side, but you got to damn near triple Steve Tasker. All I need is a little room. If I get enough room, I'm going to bring this ball back to the house, and I'm going to score." That's how confident I was.

"The only thing I need you guys to do," I told my teammates in the special teams meeting, "is make sure Steve Tasker is blocked. You put two men over him and then slide a linebacker out to chip to make sure he stays locked in. If we can contain this guy, I'll take care of the other one. I'll make the other guy miss… but you cannot let Steve get downfield. Give me a chance to make a play. If you give me a chance—just a chance—it's going to be a special day for the Rams, baby."

The guys got hyped and believed in what I was saying. They said, "Yeah, yeah, yeah, V. Okay, we got it. We got it. Stay on Tasker."

During the pre-game warm-up, I had my game face on. Usually, I don't talk to people. I have a pre-game mentality that's not very pleasant. When I was at the top of my game, I played pissed off. I didn't like anyone—not even my own people. Even when I got ready for the game, the trainers knew not to speak to me. No one dared speak to VT. I just had that mentality. Hell, I just about played with bad intentions. I was already in my mode, and playing against a team that had cut me made it even more intense. I was so focused for that game that I didn't even hear my former teammates when they said, "Hey, VT!" It didn't mean anything to me.

I can recall the very first punt return. I was excited because we had a game plan. I think we stopped them on their own twenty-two-yard line. They had to punt the ball off to me, and I just stared them down as I ran out onto the field. I said to myself, "I'm scoring," and I believed that. I saw my guys lining up. Steve Tasker was on the right-hand side. I didn't know who was on the other side on their team, but the only person I was concerned about was Steve Tasker. I was pacing from side to side, just waiting for them to punt the ball to me. When they finally kicked the ball, I said to myself, "Yeah, baby, this is going to the house. I'm scoring on this play."

There are several things a punt returner does while the ball is in the air besides psyching himself up to catch and run. The first thing he does is locate the direction of the ball. As soon as the ball gets off the punter's foot, the returner immediately runs to align himself up to the football, wherever that ball is. That's the first thing he does, and he does that as quickly as possible so he can set himself up and monitor what's going down on the field with one quick glance. That's why the first course of business for a punt returner is always to find the ball. So, I immediately found the flight of the ball, got underneath it, and waited.

The next thing a returner does is find out where there is the most dangerous guy. The returner should've already picked that individual out before the ball is ever punted. You immediately locate that guy and find out what his status is. So, when the ball got punted, I found the flight of the ball, got underneath it, set myself up, and then looked down and found Steve Tasker. There were two guys on him, and it didn't look like he was getting away, so I looked back up to find the flight of the ball. I adjusted my body again and looked to see if Tasker was still hemmed up. I saw our linebacker slide out to block him. They still had him contained, and the ball was up there pretty high, so I was able to look back up and do a small adjustment again. Something told me to look again, but I didn't because I said to myself, "They got him. There's no way Tasker is getting by those guys."

They hemmed him up, and I was about to score. All I had to do was just make my first two steps. I never looked back down, and that turned out to be a major mistake. As soon as I caught that ball, Steve Tasker's helmet was in my chest, and my back expanded out like a balloon. He hit me so hard that I flew back about four to five yards in midair. Thank God I held onto the ball. It was that hit that earned me a spot in the NFL's hardest hits video archives. I immediately got up and started talking trash to Steve. I said, "Steve, is that all you got? Is that all you got, baby? I'm coming right back. I'll be right back. If that's all you got, you're in trouble. You're in big trouble." It was such a crushing hit, and when I watched the tapes later, I could not believe I held on to the ball and started talking trash to that man who nailed me like that. It was a good game for me personally, even though we gave it up to the Bills in the end.

Steve Tasker helped me make the NFL's hardest hits video!

That Monday, we had a team meeting. Coach Knox came in and said, "Man, we had a chance to win that game. We had a game plan. We got a return man that's running for his damn life out there, and I'll tell you what, if I EVER see my return man get hit like that again, somebody's getting fired." He had tears in his eyes because he was so passionate about what he was saying. I guess Tasker hit me harder than I thought, and it was kind of impressive to me that the coach would see how hard I was working to make something happen. The coach was as pissed off as I was that my team let me take a hit like that.

It was kind of embarrassing having the coach get on everyone's case because of me getting hit, but from that moment on, I was considered one of the toughest small guys in the NFL. To take a hit like that and then get up and start talking trash and then finish the game is the type of label an athlete wants and strives for. An athlete wants a tough reputation, and Steve Tasker ensured that I got one. I was tough, no ifs, ands, or buts about it!

Chapter 35:
A Lion's Share of Issues in Detroit (1993)

I had a sub-par season that year with the Rams. In fact, at the end of the season, about the fourteenth game, I was somehow distracted, even though I wasn't sure why. I was inconsistent in my decision-making out on the football field, and I didn't have any close relationships with any of the new coaches. The bottom line is that I wasn't producing, and Chuck Knox made the decision to release me. I couldn't really blame him at the time, and I didn't have a defense; my mind was elsewhere. Looking back, I think I was just tired.

Almost immediately after being released from the Rams, probably within a week, the Detroit Lions called my agent and said they wanted to sign me right away. That's when I started my career as a Lion, and that's also when I met perhaps the second- or third-best running back ever to lace up a pair of cleats. Walter Payton is number one, in my opinion, if you haven't figured that out already, but Gayle Sayers was number two, and coming in at number three was the amazing Barry Sanders of Detroit.

I'm going to be perfectly honest with you: I wasn't too keen on the city of Detroit in general. It felt kind of dreary. Hell, it seemed damn near depressing for me. But I set that aside, because the most important thing for me was having the opportunity to continue my pro career, and working with and learning from some real quality players like Barry Sanders, Rodney Peete, Herman Moore, Brett Perriman, Willie Green, Chris Spielman, and Benny Blades was an added bonus.

Coach Wayne Fontes, however, was a different story. In my opinion, the man was more of a political figure than an actual coach. He spent more time on the golf cart with a cigar in his mouth than actually coaching. He said all the right things at the right time, and he was well liked among the players. He tried to be a player's coach, but I never saw him that way, and unfortunately, I really didn't learn much from him because of that. Still, though,

I do thank him for giving me the opportunity to move on with my career in playing for the Detroit Lions.

At the time, the Lions had perhaps the best return man in the National Football League, hands down, in Mel Gray. As long as Mel Gray was healthy, no one else was doing kickoff and punt returns. That was all Mel's business, and that's what he was born to do, in my opinion. He was a fascinating returner, and anyone in the stands watching him run almost had to stand up out of utter respect. He was a really nice guy off the field also. Mel was a class act and sharp dresser, a cat that would come in with the coolest outfits. Mel was just a cool dude altogether, and he carried himself in a professional manner at all times. It was Mel's job, and I was really impressed about how he conducted himself on and off the field.

When I got there, it was cool. I had to refocus myself, get myself hungry again, and compete. We had Aubrey Matthews, Bret Perriman, Willie Green, and Herman Moore in the wide receiver positions. We ran a four wide receivers set on offense and had Rodney Peete and Andre Ware at the quarterback position. The Detroit Lions had some weapons that year and were winning games, but I found myself always just a step behind everybody, and it wasn't because of what I was doing on the football field. It had become a political situation, and I felt those politics kept me from playing, even when it was obvious and clear that I was better than a few of the guys playing in front of me. Politics had me sitting on the sidelines when I was sure I could have been making a difference, and that was frustrating for me.

Nevertheless, as disgruntled as I was by that, the following year, I again rededicated myself for the 1993 season. I promised myself that when I got back to the Detroit Lions training camp, I was going to light it up. I was going to leave NO doubt as to whether I should be playing or warming the bench, and I was going to make it obvious that the reason I wasn't playing had nothing to do with a lack of production on the field. I went home, back to New York, and got myself one of Coach Olivieri's trademark rejuvenation speeches. I was determined to make sure they had no excuse for not playing me. My mission for the 1993 season was to outright win one of the three jobs. I was going to take the kickoff and punt return job from Mel Gray or one of the receiver slots. At that time, I felt my receiver skills had gotten tremendously better. My speed and quickness were unmatched. I was ready to go, and I was at the top of my game. I was going to give them no excuse for the next go-'round. That was my mindset going into 1993. I was ready to do battle.

I went back home to start the same training regimen I had done just before entering the league, the one I learned from Sweetness himself. I did it all: the resistance work, the hill climbing, dragging tires during my sprint workouts, running in sand, and even running through the wooded field again, trying to avoid the trees. I tried to spend as much time as I could with the family, but at the same time I was determined to be prepared physically and mentally. If someone beat me outright because they were better, I could accept that, but it did not sit well with me to be sitting on the bench for the wrong reasons.

Going into training camp, it was the same group of receivers. Willie Green and Herman Moore were the two starting outside wide receivers, and Brett Perriman and Aubrey Matthews were the inside slot receivers. Jeff Campbell was there as their alternate, and he would rotate in when those guys got tired. There was Mel Gray, who was listed as a wide receiver, but he was strictly a return specialist; he didn't go in on offense. Then, there was me, the odd man out.

Going into training camp, we knew someone had to go, and so again, it was all business, I was not playing around, and I rarely cracked jokes. I was completely focused. I had to be because I knew what I was up against. There was a player that had been with the organization for a few years, and they were comfortable with him, they were comfortable with his personality, and they were comfortable with him for a couple of other reasons that I'm not going to mention. But he wasn't out-performing me. That's what I was up against. I was determined to make it obvious that if something went down, there would be people talking on my behalf to make it right.

Just like I planned and prepared for, I went through the preseason and lit it up. There was no doubt about it: I should have been on the active roster at the end of training camp. They made the final cuts, and I breathed a sigh of relief when my name wasn't called. It looked like I made the team. I went to practice that day, and everything seemed fine in regards to my status on the team.

Someone from Player Personnel came down to the field and said, "Come inside. We need to talk." He told me they were going to release me. He had that type of look in his eyes that said "V, I don't understand it myself. This is ridiculous, and I can't believe I'm doing this." I just shook my head and remained silent because I was so stunned. He said, "But we don't want you leaving town. We're going to put you up at the hotel. They're making some roster moves, and we're going to want you back."

I still couldn't say a word. I literally did not say anything. I just stared at him. It took everything in me not to shoot the messenger. I knew he was just doing his job, but as far as I was concerned, he was a part of the management team, and that management team was screwing with my career—and my family as a result. I was on edge, but I knew enough to know that the best thing I could do under the circumstances was to keep my mouth shut. I got up out of my chair and shook his hand without saying a word, and then I left.

I immediately called Tony and Howard, my agents. "Hey, Detroit just let me go," I told them. They were totally shocked and livid. They could not believe it because they knew what type of monster preseason I had. I had pretty much outplayed most of the wide receivers, and I did a damn good job on most of the kickoff and punt returns too.

My agents eventually got off the phone with me and started making phone calls to find out what was going on. My agents agreed with the guy from Player Personnel and felt they could get me back on the team after the roster moves, but I had no intention of going back there. I could not stand Detroit, I was sick of the politics, and I hated the man who I thought spearheaded them, Coach Wayne Fontes.

I had a disgusting taste in my mouth for the organization, but unfortunately, no one else showed any interest after they released me. I ended up not getting picked up by anybody else, and a week later, the Lions called me back. My agents had to work hard to convince me to go back to those sons of bitches, and when I got there, my attitude was completely different.

The only person I actually spoke to during that time was Barry Sanders; we were actual locker mates and bowling partners. Believe it or not, Barry loved junk food just as much as I did; he would sometimes invade my locker with the sole purpose of shoplifting my snacks. All kidding aside, it was an absolute honor getting my locker raided by one of the best running backs to ever play the game!

I was very untrusting of my coaches and my teammates; when I stepped on that football field, talk about someone with bad intentions! I never did anything dirty, but I never stopped until I heard the whistle, and I almost got into several fights. When I went up against defensive backs in one-on-one drills, they couldn't touch me. I was embarrassing them, but it was really nothing different from what I had been doing in training camp. The only thing that had changed was my attitude toward everyone.

Mel Gray got hurt a week after they bought me back, and here's the interesting part of it all: they deactivated that certain player they protected when they got rid of me. Instead, they activated me for the Rams game, and I had a really good game. The following week, we played the Minnesota Vikings in Minnesota. I had another "Monster" game; I capped the night by returning a punt for fifty three yards to help setup the game-winning touchdown. My performance during that game earned me the NFC (National Football Conference) Special Teams Player of the Week honors. So, I wasn't the only one wondering what the hell was going on and why I was released in the first place. I still couldn't get past what they did to me. I was just plain pissed off for that whole season.

Again, it was politics that came to bite me in the butt. It was a political move when they kept a certain person on the team and got rid of me in the process. They were more comfortable that way. I'm not going to call anybody out by name, but the people who were involved knew exactly what the deal was. I personally think Coach Wayne Fontes had a huge hand in screwing with my career, and he really did a number on me. He made my stay in the organization a miserable experience. The fans and the players, on the other hand, were great. The saddest part about leaving Detroit was that the Lions' fans treated me well and gave me much love. Likewise, my teammates were great, the only reason I kept it together at all.

There was no place else to go but UP for me!

Chapter 36:
Breathing Easier in Tampa Bay (1993-94)

There were two coaches in Detroit for whom I had a great deal of respect: Special Teams Coach, Frank Gansz, and Wide Receivers Coach, Charlie Sanders. To be perfectly honest, I didn't trust anyone else on that coaching staff.

Yes, I was disgruntled—VERY disgruntled—in Detroit. I felt like I was one of Coach Fontes's chew toys. He never made me feel welcome. The only time he spoke to me was when Mel was hurt. He would throw me one of his fake smiles and place his arm around me and act like we were longtime buddies. But then, whenever Mel was ready to play again, he would walk by me like I was a piece of cheap-ass furniture. The moment coach Fontes felt he didn't need me, he released me. For some reason, I wasn't surprised. I didn't like him and he didn't like me. We were like oil and water, and the first opportunity he got, he let me go for good.

About a day later, the Tampa Bay Buccaneers picked me up, and finally, I could exhale again and breathe easier. I even got to play in their last game of the season. Evidently, they liked how I played the game because they signed me to a two-year contract. Did I mention they were in the same conference with Detroit? That meant they knew exactly what they were getting. In Tampa Bay, I hooked up with Special Teams Coach, George Stewart, and let's just say it was a match made in heaven.

Playing for the Tampa Bay Buccaneers was a hell of an experience. I remember the one game I played right before the end of the season. I remember being on the sidelines, watching them on offense. Craig Erickson was at quarterback, and Horace Copeland and Courtney Hawkins were the receivers. Erikson called an audible at the line of scrimmage, and Horace Copeland was closest to our sidelines, so I was right there when Craig called the audible. Horace got out of his stance, and I guess he couldn't understand or didn't realize what the audible was. It was obvious he was extremely confused because Horace started scratching his helmet— yes, scratching his helmet. I didn't realize how difficult their offensive scheme was until I saw Horace Copeland scratch his helmet like that. I said to myself, "Oh my God! I'm in for a rude awakening." I did have a couple of kickoff returns that game, but it wasn't anything special. I wore the ugliest number ever (45) for that one game, and to this day, I am convinced that was why I didn't have any good returns.

Once that game was over, I had a chance to actually sit down with George Stewart and Sam Wyche. Let me tell you, those two guys made me feel at home instantly. Coach Stewart said, "Hey, I've been trying to get you for the longest time, V. You are one hell of a return man. You're one of the toughest guys I've ever seen. We need you. As soon as we saw you were available, I ran to Sam and told him, 'We gotta get this guy... Let's get him now'!" Coach Stewart said he was determined to get me on the team and his faith in me made me feel really good, especially coming off that debacle in Detroit.

When I met with Head Coach Sam Wyche, he made me feel even that much better. He said, "We got plans next year, and you're a big part of the plan. You're a heck of a football player, one of the toughest guys I've ever seen for your size. We're going to do some things." He just kept saying, "We're going to do some things," and it was like getting a massive gift from the football gods. I headed back to New York right after my meetings with my new coaches. I was rejuvenated and excited. The one thing I was extremely excited about was the fact that I would have an opportunity to play Detroit twice. Whoever said "payback is a bitch" wasn't kidding!

I went home in the off-season and took some much-needed time off. I spent a little bit more time with the family that year than I normally did because I really needed a break. I was getting mentally and physically exhausted.

I did most of my training back home in New York and also in California. I had a girlfriend out there, my fiancée at the time. I rented an apartment in California and did my training with her by my side. She was an athlete herself, so when I didn't feel like getting up in the morning to start my workouts, she encouraged me, and we worked out together. She was a tremendous help in keeping me focused. It didn't take much, though, because I pretty much knew what I had to do. She just made sure I stayed exactly on task when it came to my workouts, and her help and encouragement made a difference.

During the off-season before training camp, I received a phone call from Coach Wyche. I picked up the phone and said, "Hello."

"Hey, V.T. this is Sam Wyche. I just wanted to call and just see how you're doing, see what's going on."

I couldn't believe my ears. I thought, *What's going on? Not this again. Hell, I didn't drop any punts. Something else is going on.*

He said, "I just wanted to call you and let you know I'm real excited about having you on the team, and we're going to be doing some things with you. In fact, I just want to let you know and make sure you're okay with it." He knew before he called exactly how I was going to feel and react. "V," he said, "I just wanted to let you know we're going to be switching your position. You're going to be with the running backs now, and you're not going to be a receiver. So you go ahead and get that running back jersey you wanted."

My jaw dropped. I can't tell you how I felt. I was speechless for a moment before I said, "Okay, Coach, I can do that. I can definitely do that. You know that's my position, Coach. I appreciate the opportunity."

He said, "No, we need to do some things with you." He just kept saying, "We just need to do some things with you."

Damn! Talk about being excited! I was ready to strap on the pads right then and there. I immediately adjusted my training regimen. I wanted to put on a few more pounds and maintain my speed. So, I went a little bit heavy on the weights, and I increased my speed training. I used a heck of a lot more resistance. I started lifting heavier weights with less repetition. I did my parachutes, tire runs, and ran on the beach, everything in boots. I had a fantastic off-season and a great training camp, and I took care of business during the preseason games. During the third preseason game, I tweaked my groin a bit, but it was nothing for me to be concerned about. My cousin Derrick came to visit me from Brooklyn and was able to catch the last preseason game. That really meant a lot to me since we had kind of lost touch for a while. Derrick was the first major athlete in our family, and I truly looked up to him—I still do, as a matter of fact! Having my cousin in Tampa with me and introducing him to my teammates, showing him around where I worked, meant a great deal to both of us. I hadn't seen him in years. We were pretty close, especially after my mom passed. He was the one I went over to Brooklyn every weekend to spend time with, so having him there in Tampa with me was a beautiful thing.

The day before our last preseason game, Coach Wyche pulled me aside and informed me that he didn't want me to play in the last preseason game. He said, "Go ahead and go through the pregame warm-up and everything, but we need you for opening day. We don't want you getting hurt!"

If it were regular season, I would have played. I was a little disappointed about not playing, but I totally understood. Either way, I was just glad to be part of the Buccaneers and glad to have a coach who was finally putting some faith in me.

Catching punts at Bucs' training camp.

Taking a hand-off from Trent Dilfer in Bucs training camp.

80 yards to pay dirt!

Chapter 37:
Payback Time—Buccaneers vs. Lions (1994)

Just to rewind a little bit, all throughout training camp, I was constantly reminded that no person had ever returned a kick or a punt for a touchdown in the nineteen-year history of the Buccaneers' existence, and they believed I was the man that was going to break the unlucky streak. There were some major expectations from the coaches, teammates, the franchise, and the fans. They all felt pretty confident that history would be made in 1994 and that Vernon Turner was going to be the first man ever to return a punt or a kick for a touchdown.

It was perhaps the most difficult football season I had. The hardest off-season I had was preparing to go to the NFL, and this was the second hardest. I knew I was physically and mentally prepared. They even did a big story on me during training camp in regards to me being the first one to make history for the franchise in returning a punt or kick.

There was exciting pressure being built up by everyone. George Stewart, the special teams coach, didn't have any doubt in his mind in regards to us making history. He said, "Hey, VT, I plan on beating you in that end zone once we do this. V, you need to do it against them damn Lions. You need to get your groove on against them Lions." That's all everyone was talking about. When—not if, but when.

I put so much pressure on myself, but it really didn't faze me that much. I told one reporter, "I'm not afraid to take a risk. You know, great things come when you take risks. I don't like fair catching the ball. People need to know that when they come down to cover me, they're going to have to come down fast, because it's very rare that will I would fair catch a ball. You can't make things happen when you don't run with the ball!"

I was reminded all the time that no one had broken a punt or kick for a touchdown return, and I could be the one. My special teams coach knew we had an opportunity to do that, and he was pretty excited. He knew we were more than capable of pulling it off, so that's where the added pressure came from. It was pretty wild during regular season; anytime I touched the ball, especially at home, whether it was on kickoff or punt return, the crowd would go crazy because they wanted that record broken. They wanted to witness history in the making.

Week Five arrived, and we were preparing for the Detroit Lions. I had spent a lot of time with Barry Sanders. I pretty much knew his style and his favorite running plays, so when we were preparing to face Detroit, I went over to Coach Wyche and said, "Sam, let me be Barry this week. I want to help. I really want to contribute. Look, I know all his moves. I know what he does. I know how he pauses and stops and goes and spins. I know all of that, and I can do it. Let me be Barry."

So, that whole week, I wore Number 20. For six days, I was Barry Sanders. I was working on my game and I had a mission. The coaches and players knew what had happened between the Detroit Lions and me. The coaches did put in some plays for me and made sure I was a part of the offensive package, which I thought was cool. I had every intention of doing something special that day, something unforgettable.

During that week of practice, I made every attempt to run just like Barry. I frustrated my teammates so much that Hardy Nicholson got pissed off at me and just threw me to the ground when we weren't supposed to go to the ground. I was already tense, and I've never been one to take any crap from anybody, no matter who it was. It must have been my New York roots, but I was a little James Cagney, especially on the football field. So what did I do? I got up, I took that ball (remember, I used to be an All-Star quarterback in high school), and I beamed it at Hardy's head. I gave him all sorts of threats, and I just snapped. I was on edge already, and I regret that I took it too far, but I was just so focused and so in tune. The coaches had to pull me aside and talk to me. They said, "Hey, V, it's not that serious."

I said, "We've got a job to do here, and he's getting mad at me for doing my job? You know it was…" I stopped mid-sentence and said, "I apologize. I did go too far, and I'll talk to Hardy later on."

That incident happened on a Wednesday, but I've got a pretty big ego for such a little guy, and I waited until Friday before talking to him. I pulled him aside and said, "Hey, man, I took it too far. I apologize, man. We cool?"

Hardy answered, "Yeah, V. You know me, man. I wear my heart on my sleeve. You did a great job this week getting us ready for Barry, and I appreciate you. I just got pissed off because... well, you know, I'm a competitor. Even at practice, I don't want anybody running all over us, which is what you were doing."

I said, "Ah, man. Hey, I just want us to be right, man. I just want us to be ready for Barry because we all know how Barry is. He's an unbelievable back, and I'm not Barry."

I'm about to make history on this play!

He said, "V, I'll tell you what... if you were a little bit thicker, you could've been his clone."

Game day arrived, and I don't think I've ever been more prepared to play than I was for that Detroit Lions game. That game was by far the most important game of my life because it was extremely personal. I wasn't thinking about being the first man to return a kick for a touchdown. I wasn't thinking about any of that stuff. All I wanted to do was stick it to Coach Wayne Fontes and the Detroit Lions someway, somehow. I didn't know how I was going to do it, but I knew it was going to be done. I knew that! We went out for pre-game warm-up, and the guys from the Lions tried to talk to me.

I didn't want to hear anything from anybody, especially them. I didn't want to hear anything. I hated everybody, and I was just pissed off. Even when I was getting dressed for the game, I was extremely pissed, but the great thing about it was my teammates, my coaching staff, my trainers, and our equipment men knew how I was before a game, and they respected and embraced it. They let me be me, and they let me do me.

Because they did that, I was able to do some special things for them. I remember that game like it was yesterday. We got the ball first, and at opening kick, I guess they knew better because they kicked away from me. During the opening drive, Sam sent me in to run a sweep play, and I ran around the left side for a nine-yard gain. When I got up, I just stared at Wayne Fontes. I don't know what it was about that guy, but I just didn't like him, mostly because he treated me like crap when I played for him.

We ended up getting a field goal that drive, and then we kicked the ball off to them. On their second down, I was just looking at the field, checking to see what yard line they were on. All I was thinking about was getting enough room to catch the punt. I needed enough room, so the further back they were on the field, the more room I had to catch that punt. I had no intention of fair catching. All I needed was a little room, and then I could show Fontes what he was missing out on.

On second down, they threw an incomplete pass. Third down, they tried to run a screen play to Barry Sanders, and he didn't go anywhere. By that time, they were on their own twenty or twenty-five yard line. I was on our twenty-five, just pacing from side to side, staring at punter Greg Montgomery. It was a bizarre moment for me because I was just thinking about all the things that I went through and all the politics over in Detroit. I was thinking about all the hard work my mom and dad had done to keep me straight and how they never got to see what I had become. I was thinking about anything and everything, and then I got angry again. I started thinking about all the bad things that were done to me when I was in Detroit, and I started cussing out the punter, daring him to kick it to me. I was talking to myself, and I kept pacing from side to side. I knew Greg Montgomery, and he was an excellent punter, but he often outkicked his coverage. He was a big-time punter who went for distance more than height, so I knew I was going to get a chance to return that ball.

Prior to that, Curtis Buckley, one of the best special teams guys (next to Steve Tasker) that I've ever been around, had been saying to me all week, "V, you're going to score, baby. You're going to score. You're taking it to the house."

On fourth down, I had to go out on that football field to return the punt. Curtis looked at me as he was going on the field as well. He said, "V, this is it. This is yours now. I'll meet you in the end zone. This is yours, baby. I'm going to meet you in the end zone. This is your show."

I just looked at him and nodded my head.

Greg Montgomery punted that ball, and I could tell as soon as it got in the air that he had outkicked his coverage, he kicked it too far. He left me room to catch and run, and in that second, I was sure he had sealed his fate by kicking the ball like that. All I needed was room, and he handed it to me on a silver platter.

I don't know what it was. Usually, I would adjust my eyes down to see where the guys were that were coming down to cover me, but that time, I didn't do that. I kept my eyes on that ball the whole time, from the second it left Montgomery's foot. I said, "It doesn't matter where they're at. I'm going to return his ball! The ball is going to be returned, I'm not fair catching this ball." As soon as I caught the ball, I eluded the first guy and started high stepping toward our sidelines. I've never been a show boater, so I think it was more or less to set up my blocks. I wanted to wait until my guys got into position, so I slowed down. That, in turn, forced the defense to slow down. I knew I could go from zero to sixty faster than anybody on that field, and my stop-and-go was the best in the business.

When I paused and hesitated on my high step, I saw my guys coming to get position in their blocks, and then I shifted a gear and turned that corner, and that's all she wrote. When I turned that corner, there was only one guy to beat, Greg Montgomery and my teammate Mazio Royster lit that doggone punter up. I made a move on the inside, then busted back out, and all I saw was end zone. I think I got to the ten-yard line before I started high stepping again. I got in the end zone and did the Superman stance at the crowd. I was in another world. The first person to greet me in that end zone was my Special Teams Coach George Stewart. Hell, he damned near beat me into the end zone. That was the highlight of my career, to be honest with you, because of the timing and because of what it stood for. That moment alone made this whole crazy football career of mine even more special, just that one play. The stadium went absolutely crazy. I don't think I paid for anything in any of the restaurants I went to for the rest of the season; that's how happy the city of Tampa was for me. It was a beautiful thing, and it's something else I will never forget.

The punter watched me make history!

Chapter 38:
Bye Bye Bucs and Carolina Blues

I ended up having a really good year. I was rated one of the top return men and one of the toughest small guys in the National Football League. I gained myself a pretty decent reputation among the likes of Eric Metcalf, Dave Meggett, Mel Gray, and Brian Mitchell. When return men were mentioned, my name was right in there with those guys, and that alone was an accomplishment in itself—a true honor to be included with some of the most dynamite return men in our time.

Another memorable moment in my career was when the Buccaneers played against the Washington Redskins. The Redskins signed James Jenkins as a free agent right out of Rutgers University. We traveled to Washington in week fifteen, and talk about a huge turnout from Staten Island! It was the first and only time there had EVER been two players coming out of Curtis High School and making it in the pro ranks in the same year. I remember receiving a phone call from Coach Olivieri a few days before the game; he was so excited to see James and me competing in the NFL on the same field. Thinking back now, it was pretty damn awesome! Game time came, and like always, I had my game face on. To make a long story short, we won the game, and I had the game-breaking punt return that set up the field goal that won the game for the Bucs. I think that was the first time I'd ever seen Coach Olivieri with watery eyes!

Once the season was over, we started negotiating for a new contract. I wanted at least a three-year deal. Tampa wanted it, too, but they were about saving money, and I was about making it. Unfortunately for me, the Buccaneers and I could not come to contract terms, so I ended up signing with the Carolina Panthers to a three-year contract. I always say that everything happens for a reason, so I really don't have any regrets. I knew I was leaving with unfinished business. I wanted to get the kickoff return for a touchdown record, which I didn't get. I had a seventy-seven-yard kickoff return that year, but I didn't score.

When I signed with the Carolina Panthers, little did I know I was being put back in the same mode I was thrown into when I was with Detroit. They didn't even consider using me in their offensive scheme. I knew during that time that I had to be more than just a return specialist; I had to be used on the offensive side of the ball. It was like a bad horror movie for me when the Panthers put me back to playing wide receiver, a position I didn't want to play. I was so mentally frustrated that I didn't give myself a fair chance in making the team. They released me after the last preseason game.

Believe it or not, I ended up going back to Detroit. The Player Personnel guy said, "Look, I know you probably don't want to be back here, but the higher-ups wanted us to make this phone call. They want you back here, and whatever riff you and Coach had, it will be forgotten."

I didn't get that call until maybe the fourth or fifth game of the season, so I ended up signing with the Lions. Hell, it was the same crap, different day, and nothing changed.

When that season was over, I re-signed with the Tampa Bay Buccaneers, but Coach Sam Wyche was gone. He was the only coach that had seen firsthand what I could actually do, so I wasn't too happy about him not being there. They had hired Tony Dungy as head coach and Mike Schuler as the offensive coordinator. Right from the start, it wasn't a good fit at all. Coach Schuler was pretty much set on who he wanted and where he wanted them, and there was no room for me in Tampa anymore. I made it up to the last cut, but they ended up releasing me.

Chapter 39:
Life after the NFL

About a month later, I wasn't sure if I wanted to play anymore. I was physically and mentally exhausted, and that's putting it lightly. I got sick and tired of the business side of the game. I don't know what it was about them damn Detroit Lions, and I couldn't believe they wanted me back there again. I had no clue why. I was seriously considering putting on the Honolulu blue, silver, black, and white again, but about a month before training camp, just when I was about to sign their contract, I woke up one day, sat on the side of my bed, and said, "I've had enough. I'm done." The thought of going back to that organization literally made my skin crawl. It was then, in 1996, that I decided to end my NFL career.

I decided I wanted to do some traveling, but I was kind of frugal and didn't want to pay for it. I got in touch with NFL Europe. I thought I could play some ball, have some fun, and they would take care of all the travelling and expenses. So, I ended up doing that for two years. It was an awesome, unforgettable experience. I traveled all throughout Europe for two years.

Unfortunately, that trip ended up being the demise of my marriage. I got married in 1995, and by 1999, I was divorced. We were having some issues even before I decided to travel abroad. As many couples sadly do, we had simply grown apart, and that was one of the main reasons I wanted to travel; I wanted to run away from my problems, and I know now that it was a mistake. She was a good woman, but evidently, she wasn't the woman for me.

I had enjoyed a tremendous career under the circumstances. My family stayed together and was taken care of. I had the opportunity to travel throughout the United States and abroad. I met some unbelievable people throughout my eight-year pro career. I really had no business playing professional football and doing the things that I accomplished, but it's amazing what hard work and determination can do.

Becoming mentally and physically drained was a huge factor in my decision to retire. I was truly anti-football for several years after that. In fact, for a change of pace, my career after football was in the office furniture installation industry, where I worked for three years. After that, I took an opportunity to work in the tire manufacturing industry for almost nine years. During my first couple of years with the tire manufacturing company, I met a guy by the name of Terrence Martin. He worked in the Human Resources Department and he's the one that actually hired me.

I'm sure everyone has come across a person that made an instant impression—a person you knew would become a friend for life. Terrence was that guy for me. I don't think I will ever come across another person with a bigger heart, a person that goes out of his way to pay it forward every chance he gets. I am so proud to call him my friend. Thanks to Terrence, I got the opportunity to change my career once again from the tire manufacturing industry to the oil refining industry in Houston, Texas, and as a result, I can honestly say I've been blessed ten times over.

I guess my competitive nature will always keep me involved in athletics in some form or fashion. I try to keep myself in good shape; in fact, on my forty-third birthday, I went out to the park down the street from my house, and measured out forty yards. I ran two forties; the first one was a 4.51 and the second one was a 4.48. My goal is to be able to break under 4.5 at age fifty. And, yes, it's an ego thing.

After retirement, I relieved my gridiron itch by playing in adult flag football leagues. In the year 2000, I developed, directed, and participated in a league (AFFL) in Mount Vernon, Illinois. The league became one of the most productive adult programs in the southern Illinois region. The younger athletes had mercy on this old guy and let me score a touchdown or two. Nowadays, you can find me on the golf course, still trying to get a ball in for the score.

Coaching in a play-off game with Mt. Vernon H.S.

Talking to Coach Olivieri during my visit at Curtis H.S.

Talking to the Curtis H.S. football team.

My family.

Chapter 40:
I Couldn't Have Done It Without You

There are so many people I need to me
me during my whole athletic career.
of a ride; hell, it was a storybook ride. The thing I
want to point out in this book is that we're going to have our ob-
stacles and tragedies in life, but that's part of life. Quitting is not
an option. Walter Payton said it best: "Never die easy… always
die hard!" To this day, I'm living my life to the fullest. If I'm going
to fail in something, I'm going to fail trying, and I'm going to fail
hard!

The message of this book is to let people know that life is tough.
It really is, but if you truly put your mind to something and don't
give up, and if you keep fighting, during the course of that fight,
doors will be slammed in your face, but other doors of opportunity
will open. You don't know when or where, but another door is going to open, and that door is most likely the door you're supposed
to be going through to get to where you need to be. My parents really didn't raise any quitters. I didn't have an option; I had to fight.
But I didn't do it by myself…

To my parents… You were unbelievable parents. You taught
us never to quit, to always stick together, and you made so many
sacrifices for us. Not a day goes by that I don't think of you. Mom
and Dad, from all of your kids, we thank you.

To my brothers and sisters, Jemal, Sharlene, Brian, and Ellen…
I just want to thank you for being you. I could not have completed
this project without you guys! No one will ever truly understand
nor feel what we went through. It was one hell of a journey. We
had our issues and our problems and arguments, including our
sibling rivalries, but when push comes to shove, we're going to
be there for one another. We all went through hell, but we made
it. We stayed together, the Fab Five! I would be doing Jeff Burkey
and James Crawford a major injustice if I didn't mention them be-

e these guys are family as well. They practically grew up in ur house. They are also our brothers, and they are a huge part of me. I love you guys.

To Coach Fred Olivieri… If you read the book in its entirety, you would know you were not only my football coach, but you also became one of my best friends and someone I completely relied on. I also must thank your wife, Joan, for making me feel so welcome in your home; you are one of the sweetest ladies I have had the pleasure of knowing! Coach, your daughter, Elise, and your son, Jeff, grew up right before my eyes. It's hard to believe they're both adults now! Fred, your father, was always a big VT fan. I never told you this, but he used to give me ten bucks every time he saw me, and he'd say in a whispery voice, "Here, put this in your pocket, and don't tell Coach." Your family was easy to love, Coach! I could never repay you for what you have done for me and my family. You have been my lifeline, Fred; I thank you from the bottom of my heart!

To my Assistant Coach, Bob McGhie… You've always been there when I needed you. I also watched your kids, Jason and Lea, grow up. You were a good coach, and you were and still are a fantastic father to your kids. Thank you, Bobby… just for being you.

To my Assistant Coach, Jim McKeon… Thank you for the respect and support during my high school career. I loved the way you got us going before a game.

To my agents, Tony Agnone and Howard Shatsky… You guys really took care of me during my career. You taught me the business, mental, and political sides of the game before I ever entered a training camp, and I can't thank the two of you enough.

To Coach Bill Thatcher… In the short amount of time that I've known you, there's only one other person that had more of an impact in my athletic career and my life. I remember quitting your

Pop Warner football team due to my situation at home. I also remember you tracking me down in the park to speak with me. In that conversation, you taught me how to use my aggression on the field. You taught me how to block distractions out of my mind, to flip that switch, and never to quit. I actually listened to you because I trusted you. Coach Thatcher, you never gave up on me, and you didn't allow me to give up on myself. I look back now and wonder what would've happened if you hadn't tracked me down that day. I wonder how my life would've turned out had I not listened to your advice. The alternative result is a frightening thought. Just thinking about what you did for me all those years ago brings tears to my eyes. Coach Thatcher, from the bottom of my heart, thank you.

To Coach Bob Andrews... Though I only had one track season with you, that one year was an incredible one for me. I absolutely loved your competitive edge; your energy was truly contagious. You taught me to destroy my opponents with my actions, not with my words. You made my one year in track a productive and memorable one. You're one hell of a track coach and human being. Thank you, Coach Andrews.

To Troy McGhie... Hey man, you have been by my side during the highs and lows of my life. We just clicked from the first day we met! You and your wife, Chris, have been a life line for me; you and your family have become a huge part of my life. When God bought you into my life, He blessed me with an unconditional friend, someone who stood by my side through it all! Love you, man!!!

To Coaches Ken Sparks, Dennis Webb, and Mike Turner... Coach Ken Sparks, your outlook on life and your ability to get the most out of us was the main reason why I decided to attend Carson-Newman College. Coaches Dennis Webb and Mike Turner, your genuine nature and your firm, but nurturing mentality, was the reason I stayed at Carson-Newman.

To my additional coaches: Dan Reeves, Marv Levy, John Robinson, Jimmy Raye Sr., Wayne Fontes, Charles Sanders, Frank Gansz, Sam Wyche, George Stewart, Dom Capers, Ernie Stautner (R.I.P), and Jim Criner... All of you gave me my opportunities during my pro career. Thank you.

To my close friends: Troy McGhie (and family), Roberto Infante, James Jenkins, Phil Garner, Josh Aycott, John Roda, Peter McNamara, Mike Almestica, Juanita Almestica, Cynthia Santiago, Horace Smith, Hadiyah Anderson, James Haynes, Jim Wlcek (and family), Rick Halbach, Mike Lopez, Lynda Hill (and family), Edwin Lowery, David Pool, Joe Fishback, Sammy Dixon, Ray Butler, Robert Thomas, Larry Ryans, Jimmy Raye (and family), Barry Sanders, Jim Kelly, Susan Morss, Mike Carbonaro, Jason Ohley, Tonya Cooley, Al Williams, Matt Gajewski (and family), Anita Day, Bobby Phillips, Jason Pace, Kevin and Tracy Devoy, Lorena Banda, Mark Spikes, Marinda Simmons, Mike Blakemore, Orlena Rogers (and family)Thomas Bingley, Jason Quinn, Shauanna Charbonnet, Ron Harlow, Mike Irwin, Barbara Prideaux, Jennifer Held and Margarita Santiago, and Steve Shapiro... You have all made a lasting impression in my life and I thank you!

To my teammates at Curtis High: James Jenkins, John Roda, Phil Garner, Josh Aycott, George Brown, Robert Talley, Sam Litrell, Glen Nardiello, Mike Bellantoni, Pete McNamara, Tom Mitchell, Tyrone Paniss, Gabe Mokwauh, Mike Lopez, David Cress, Warren Williams, and Todd Turner.... No one can be successful in team sports without having good teammates. I was able to break all sorts of records in high school, and none of those records could have been broken if it wasn't for your help. Not only were you guys great teammates, but you were also my friends. Thank you.

To my teammates at Carson-Newman: Edwin Lowery, Pat Johnson, David Mack, Ken Tyson, Robert Thomas, Ray Butler, Chad Sparks, Jeff Simms, Mark Johnson, Buster Goins, Joe Fishback, Brent Collins, Sammy Dixon, Vernon Anderson, and David

Pool... Who would have thought a kid from New York would spend his college years in the South? Having great teammates made my stay a memorable one, and I thank each and every one of you for those memories.

To my teammates in the NFL: Shannon Sharpe, Vance Johnson, John Elway, James Lofton, Andre Reed, Bruce Smith, Darryl Talley, Thurman Thomas, Jim Kelly, 'Mr. Steve Tasker,' Carlton Bailey, Al Edwards, Henry Ellard, Flipper Anderson, Aaron Cox, Jimmy Raye, Sam Lilly, Kevin Greene, Jackie Slater, Larry Ryans, Barry Sanders, Herman Moore, Brett Perriman, Willie Green, Chris Spielman, Lomas Brown, Aubrey Matthews, Willie Clay, Andre Ware, Rodney Peete, Mel Gray, Mike, Husted, Mazio Royster, Curtis Buckley, Hardy Nickerson, Trent Dilfer, Craig Erickson and Derrick Brooks... I came across some amazing athletes and some unique characters during my pro career. Thank you, guys, for showing me how to play this game at the highest level!

To my right-hand lady, Rachelle Clinton... There is no way I could have pulled this project off without your help, dear friend. You were a godsend, without a doubt! I could not have chosen a better person to help launch this book. You're an unbelievable young lady, and I'm eternally grateful to you.

There are probably countless others I have forgotten to mention here, and I truly apologize. Just know that you're never forgotten in my heart. You all have been a huge part of what I am and what I became.

2010 visit to Staten Island Hall of Fame.

Closing Thoughts

I don't like to say I'm lucky; I am blessed to have been able to take advantage of the opportunities that were given to me. I will continue working with young athletes, not only to make a positive impression in their athletic career, but most importantly, to have a positive influence in their lives. Paying it forward is something I simply have to do because I have been so blessed. I hope this book will be viewed as a positive testimony to never quit, because amazing things can happen when you persevere to the next level. Great things come when you take a risk, and I am living proof of that. Leaving my mark and making a difference is extremely important to me. Everyone needs to ask themselves, "If I die today, how would I be remembered?"

God bless,

Vernon Maurice Turner
http://www.VernonTurner.com
Website Includes: additional photos, training regimen support, book reviews, and contact information.

Credits

Photography Credits

Cover action photography:
- Used with permission of the Orlando Sentinel, Copyright 2010.
- Used with permission of the Associated Press, Copyright 2010.

Cover still photography:
- Rachelle Clinton

Additional Credits

Transcriber:
- Always On Time Virtual Administrative Services

Proofreader and Copy Editor:
- Autumn J. Conley
- Gianna Carini

Agent/Advisor:
- Howard Shatsky
  Professional Football Management

VT's Ten Commandments

1. Show love and respect to your parents at ALL times… They can be gone in a blink of an eye!

2. Always outwork your opponent; if you know you've outworked your opponent, chances are you'll outplay them!

3. Focus on the weak part of your game to become a more complete athlete.

4. NEVER cut corners; if you start something, FINISH it! Every athlete must pay their dues!

5. The way you practice is the way you will play; if you develop bad habits when you're preparing, there's a very good chance it will carry over in games!

6. ALWAYS respect your opponent; every good athlete loves to be underestimated!

7. When you lead by example, you will be one of the most powerful and productive leader in the world! "What you do speaks so well that no one needs to hear what you have to say"

8. Always have respect and loyalty to your teammates, coaches, and the program… in that order!

9. Your body is your temple; stay in shape at all times… you never know when your number will be called… **NO DRUGS!**

10. Be an ambassador; always present yourself with class, on and off the field, because like it or not ,you're a role model for all the other young athletes and they see EVERYTHING you do! And always… **PAY IT FORWARD!**